**Oryx Sourcebook Series
in Business and Management**

Marketing and Sales Management

An Information Sourcebook

Oryx Sourcebook Series in Business and Management

Paul Wasserman, Series Editor

**Oryx Sourcebook Series
in Business and Management**

Marketing and Sales Management
An Information Sourcebook

by Jean Herold
Business Librarian/Bibliographer
University of Texas, Austin

Phoenix • New York
ORYX PRESS
1988

The rare Arabian Oryx is believed to have inspired the myth of the unicorn. This desert antelope became virtually extinct in the early 1960s. At that time several groups of international conservationists arranged to have 9 animals sent to the Phoenix Zoo to be the nucleus of a captive breeding herd. Today the Oryx population is over 400, and herds have been returned to reserves in Israel, Jordan, and Oman.

Copyright © 1988 by
The Oryx Press
2214 North Central at Encanto
Phoenix, AZ 85004-1483

Published simultaneously in Canada

Printed and Bound in the United States of America

∞ The paper used in this publication meets the minimum requirements of American National Standard for Information Science—Permanence of Paper for Printed Library Materials, ANSI Z39.48, 1984.

Library of Congress Cataloging-in-Publication Data

Herold, Jean.
  Marketing and sales management : an information sourcebook / by Jean Herold.
    p. cm. — (Oryx sourcebook series in business and management ; no. 12)
  Includes index.
  ISBN 0-89774-406-3
  1. Marketing—United States—Management—Bibliography. 2. Sales management—United States—Bibliography. 3. Marketing—Information services—United States—Directories. 4. Selling—Information services—United States—Directories. I. Title. II. Series
Z7164.M18H46 1988
[HF5415.13]
658.8—dc19   87-32444

Contents

Introduction

Marketing has no single, accepted definition because of the diversity of perspectives. Some definitions highlight consumer demand, sales motivation, distribution of goods, or services for profit. Some relate marketing to time creation and possession utilities, others to delivery of a standard of living or activities that facilitate and consummate exchanges. Whatever the definition, the marketing function involves economic activity covering areas such as product development, packaging, market research, advertising, sales promotion, distribution, and franchising, retailing, direct marketing, service marketing, and nonprofit marketing.

Marketing is also recognized as a major factor in our economy. Almost every type of business and nonprofit organization is concerned with selling its products or services, and vast resources are devoted to this process. Although marketing provides and supports millions of jobs, its cost affects goods or services because a large percentage of the price reflects marketing costs. This is an important consideration for the marketing manager.

To successfully market a product or service at a fair price, the marketing strategy of an organization is based on careful planning. Relevant internal and external information is essential for marketing decisions. Internal information is available in organization records and is usually easy to obtain. External marketing information is in a wide variety of sources, and the problem is identifying these sources. This bibliography is designed to provide a list of these external marketing information sources.

SCOPE

Intended for the business person, researcher, student, librarian, or the person interested in marketing or selling of goods and services, the focus of this sourcebook is on management techniques and practical aspects of marketing and sales as practiced in the United States. International marketing is not included.

The suggested titles provide a variety of viewpoints from the business community and the academic world, with some practically oriented and others theoretically oriented. The books are limited to English-language materials primarily published from 1980 to the present. Exceptions are made if there are no later publications to cover the subject. Only a few textbooks are included. Generally, the books are commercially available and are located in academic, special, and some public libraries.

A list of relevant journal titles are included in most of the chapters. The numerous trade journals and newsletters for specific types of businesses are not included. The directories of periodicals, serials, and newsletters listed in the chapter Marketing—General have complete lists of these types of publications.

No journal articles are cited because online or CD-ROM databases provide up-to-date information on specific business topics. Older information is also available on these databases because some have indexed articles from as early as 1971. Full-text databases have the entire article online for viewing or printing a copy.

Marketing reports on products and industries produced by marketing research firms are not listed. These reports are usually expensive and have a limited time span of relevancy. For names of the companies providing this service, see the directories listed in the chapter Marketing Research.

Retailing has selective coverage because there are so many types of retail outlets. For information sources and periodicals for retail businesses not included in this bibliography, check the *Encyclopedia of Business Information Sources.*

Databases provide the most efficient method of manipulating a tremendous amount of data/information to locate items specifically suited to one's needs. This information includes commercial data that are previously printed; public data, which are government-collected information; and private data, which relate to companies. The types of information in databases are bibliographic, which include citations/abstracts/full text of articles and reports, and nonbibliographic, which is numeric or directory-type information.

The selective listing of databases is necessitated by the increasing proliferation of online systems and databases developed and marketed. The databases included in this bibliography are limited to those online systems found in most libraries—BRS Information Technologies (BRS); DIALOG Information Services, Inc. (DIALOG); Mead Data Central, Inc. (NEXIS); and VU/TEXT Information Services, Inc.

The more complex database protocols are being simplified, and some of the systems provide a menu-driven, user-friendly search mode that anyone, with the proper equipment, can search for needed information. Reduced rates for online searching on BRS/BRKTHRU, which includes all of the BRS databases, are provided during the day and at night, while BRS/AFTERDARK, which has a limited number of databases, is available only after business hours. DIALOG has Business Connection, developed for the end user, covering products, markets, financial data, and sales prospecting in selected business databases. KNOWLEDGE INDEX, another DIALOG database, includes selected databases in business and other areas and is available at a reduced rate after business hours. For information on additional databases and systems, see the database directories listed in the chapter Marketing—General, which includes description, access, and cost information for the numerous databases now available.

Technology is also providing marketing information in new formats. Information Access Company has developed INFOTRAC, which uses an IBM PC to search the monthly updated database on laser disc. The emphasis is on the business topics. Another development is the Compact Disk Read Only Memory or CD-ROM, used by DATEXT for its database, which provides information on 10,000 public companies in consumer, industrial, service, and technology areas and uses a personal computer for searching. ABI/Inform, a bibliographic database, is testing a CD-ROM format in 1987.

ARRANGEMENT

This bibliography is divided into marketing topics. The chapter Marketing—General includes basic sources for all areas of marketing. If a book covers several topics, it is generally included in this chapter. Most of the databases are listed here also. Those that are specific to a topic are listed in that chapter.

The books cited are arranged by format of the book. The divisions are obvious except for the Guidebooks/Handbooks designation. This is a liberal interpretation and includes how-to books, manuals, explanatory texts with procedures outlined, reviews of procedures, methods or techniques. These generally have a practical viewpoint, but scholarly treatments are also included. The Papers—Collection sections list books of readings or journal articles that provide an overview of the subject area.

CORE COLLECTION

Selection of titles for the core collection is difficult because of the needs of different organizations and the cost of books and journals. Many of the serial titles are expensive and require an annual purchase to have the latest information, which is desirable for marketing plans. Books also tend to go out of print, and older titles are not always available for purchase. Interpretation of the importance of a particular title is subjective and may not be what someone else would choose. A collection may not require all of the titles or may require even more in an area because of a particular emphasis. With all these caveats, the list represents the basic areas in the bibliography.

Abbreviations

ADI   - Area of Dominant Influence

CMSA   - Consolidated Metropolitan Statistical Area

MSA   - Metropolitan Statistical Area

PIMS   - Profit Impact of Marketing Strategy

SIC   - Standard Industrial Classification

SMSA   - Standard Metropolitan Statistical Area

Marketing and Sales Management

Marketing—General

ABSTRACTS

1. *Business Publications Index and Abstracts.* Monthly with annual cumulations. Prepared by Management Contents. Detroit, MI: Gale Research Co. 2 pts.

Periodicals, proceedings, transactions, self-study course, some newsletters, and books are indexed in this publication which is the printed duplicate of MANAGEMENT CONTENTS, an online database. Divided into two parts, the monthly index lists subject and author citations and has brief abstracts for the entries. The abstract section does not cumulate because each abstract has a unique number, and citations are to these numbers. The subject/author index has an annual cumulation.

2. *Management & Marketing Abstracts.* Monthly. Elmford, NY: Pergamon Press.

Aimed at the management and marketing executive, the index covers areas of marketing as well as topics on management and planning. Theoretical and practical information is indexed from a worldwide selection of 130 relevant publications.

3. *Marketing & Distribution Abstracts.* 8/yr. Wembley, England: Anbar Publications Ltd.

Published in association with the Institute of Marketing in England, this current awareness service lists recent articles in British and American journals alphabetically by the title of the journal, not the subject. This publication is intended for a quick overview of recently published articles.

4. *Marketing Doctoral Dissertations Abstracts.* Annual. Chicago: American Marketing Assn., 1975–.

The two-page abstracts of marketing doctoral dissertations, published as a part of the AMA Bibliography Series, is not very current because the 1983 volume covers 1981 dissertations. The online database Dissertation Abstracts International provides more up-to-date coverage of marketing dissertations.

5. *Monthly Catalog of U.S. Government Publications.* Monthly. Washington, DC: U.S. Government Printing Office.

This publication lists federal government publications by agency. The information covers a wide range of subjects including studies, reports, statistical data, and periodical publications on business topics. Subject, keyword and report number indexes are in each monthly issue. An annual *Serials Supplement* lists the documents that are continuously published. Online searching of this publication is available.

6. *Predicasts Marketing Update.* Weekly. Cleveland, OH: Predicasts, Inc.
Abstracts material on topics such as market analysis and testing, new product introductions, promotions and sales techniques, market research, consumer regulations, sales compensation, and demographic trends. More than 1,300 business and government sources are scanned for relevant material.

7. *PROMT: Predicasts Overview of Markets and Technology.* Monthly. Cleveland, OH: Predicasts, Inc.
More than 4,000 abstracts from over 100 sources are included in each monthly issue, with indexes cumulated quarterly and annually. The articles cover major industry categories including new products and technology, research, market trends, sales and shipment data, management, and industry news.

8. *Psychological Abstracts.* Monthly. Washington, DC: American Psychological Assn.
Abstracts of a broad range of psychological research cover advertising, behavior, and some aspects of marketing.

BIBLIOGRAPHIES

9. Madden, Charles S., et al., eds. *Annotated Bibliography of Marketing Education 1975–1984.* n.p.: Southern Marketing Assn.,1986. 71 p.
For those interested in marketing education, this bibliography lists articles from refereed journals and association proceedings, including conceptual and empirical papers on a variety of topics such as pedagogical issues, curriculum, and computer applications. Category and author indexes are provided.

10. Robinson, Larry M., and Adler, Roy D. *Marketing Megawords: The Top 150 Books and Articles.* Westport, CT: Praeger, 1987. 211 p.
Summaries and evaluations of books that are judged to have the most impact on the marketing discipline are included in this book. Forty-six selections are based on citation analysis; others are winning articles and articles frequently mentioned in anthologies or collections of classics. The summaries are alphabetically arranged by author, with separate indexes by author and by title for books and articles, and by date of publication. The top twenty articles and books are ranked by citation frequency.

DATABASE DIRECTORIES

11. Cotton, Marya. *Executive's Sourcebook to Marketing, Company and Demographic Data: A Directory to On-Line, Off-Line, Data Tapes and Diskettes from Commercial Vendors, State Government Offices, Federal Agencies and Non-Profit Organizations.* Chevy Chase, MD: Information USA, Inc., 1986. 403 p.
More than 1,800 computerized data sources cover company information, market share, and other marketing data. A detailed index provides access to the exact data needed.

12. *Database Directory 1984/85.* White Plains, NY: Knowledge Industry Publications, 1984. 437 p.
An alphabetical listing of machine-readable databases available for public access in the U.S. and Canada that includes basic information, corresponding printed sources, and search aids. Separately paged vendor, producer, and subject indexes are provided.

13. *Datapro Complete Guide to Dial-Up Databases.* Loose-leaf. Delron, NJ: Datapro Research Corp., 1985–.

More than 2,000 publicly accessible databases are arranged alphabetically with each citation covering information about scope, update, conditions of usage, pricing, training, and installation. A subject index and user ratings are included in this loose-leaf format.

14. *Directory of Online Databases.* Quarterly. New York: Quadra/Elsevier, 1987.

The quarterly issues of this directory supersede the previous issues to provide current information on more than 2,800 databases which are arranged alphabetically. Each entry includes basic information. Separate indexes are by subject, producer, online gateways/services, telecommunications, and a master index for all of these.

15. *The Federal Data Base Finder.* 2d ed. Potomac, MD: Information USA, Inc., 1987. 368 p.

More than 4,000 free and fee-based databases are divided into three sections—those directly online through federal agencies, contractors, or centers; commercial databases containing government supplied data; and computer tapes sold by the federal government. Basic information about each includes the contact agency or producer.

16. Lucas, Amy F., and Marcaccio, Kathleen Young. *Encyclopedia of Information Systems and Services.* 7th ed. Detroit, MI: Gale Research Co., 1985. 3 vols. 1,200 p.

Detailed descriptions of 2,700 entries for U.S. organizations are in volume one, and more than 1,250 entries for organizations in other countries are in volume two. These organizations produce and/or provide access to computerized information in all subject areas and include database producers and publishers, online vendors, computer time-sharing companies, and fee-based information services. Seventeen points of information are in each citation with twenty-seven indexes provided in volume three. *New Information Systems and Services* are periodic updating supplements for this directory.

17. Mayros, Van, and Michael, Werner D. *Data Bases for Business: Profiles and Applications.* Radnor, PA: Chilton Book Company, 1982. 178 p.

Part one is an introduction to database retrieval systems and how to get started. Part two is an alphabetically arranged directory with basic information including a profile or description of information in the database, applications, and online vendor service. Part three has subject, producer, and vendor indexes.

18. *The North American Online Directory: A Directory of Information Products and Services with Names and Numbers.* New York: Bowker, 1985. 265 p.

This trade directory includes alphabetical listings of online vendors, producers and their products, telecommunication networks, library networks and consortia, information collections and analysis centers, consultants, and associations. Subject indexes and a bibliography of relevant reference books, periodicals, and newsletters are included.

19. Schmittroth, John; Maxfield, Doris Morris; and Lucas, Amy F. *Online Database Search Services Directory: A Reference and Referral Guide to Libraries, Information Firms, and Other Sources Providing Computerized Information Retrieval and Associated Services Using Publicly Available Online Databases.* Detroit, MI: Gale Research Co., 1984. 2 vols. 1,187 p.

Detailed information on libraries, information firms, and other organizations that provide computerized information retrieval and associated services is provided.

Indexes are by organization name, online systems accessed, subject, databases searched, search personnel, and geographic location.

20. Williams, Martha E.; Lannom, Laurence; and Robins, Carolyn G., eds. *Computer-Readable Databases: A Directory and Data Source Book: Business, Law, Humanities, Social Sciences.* Vol. 2. Chicago: American Library Assn., 1985. pp. 420–1,029.
> This latest issue contains 2,805 databases arranged alphabetically by name, with basic information about the database including subject, scope, and user aids noted. Separately paged indexes include name, subject, producer, and processor.

SELECTED DATABASE VENDORS

The vendors listed below provide online database access for many libraries. All of the databases included in this book are available from one or another of these vendors. For additional information, use the toll-free telephone numbers.

21. BRS Information Technologies (BRS). 1200 Route 7, Latham, NY 12110 (800-345-4277).

22. DIALOG Information Services, Inc. (DIAL). 3460 Hillview Ave., Palo Alto, CA 94304 (800-387-2689).

23. Mead Data Central (MEAD). P.O. Box 933, Dayton, OH 45401 (800-227-4908).

24. VU/TEXT (VU). 1211 Chestnut St., Philadelphia, PA 19107 (800-258-8080).

DATABASES

Online

This list of databases covers general marketing topics and includes the beginning date of coverage, the name of the database producer, and the vendors' names. Additional databases that are useful for a specific topic are listed in other chapters. The database directories provide a detailed explanation of each database and list additional database vendors.

25. ABI/INFORM. 1971–. Louisville, KY: Data Courier, Inc. (Vendors: BRS, DIAL, MEAD, VU)
> Abstracts of articles from more than 550 business journals, primarily from the U.S. with some Canadian and European materials included. Covers all areas of business, including marketing research and advertising.

26. Arthur D. Little/Online. 1971–. Cambridge, MA: Arthur D. Little Resources. (Vendor: DIAL)
> Reports on industries, technology, and management topics include economic forecasts, consumer products and services, opinion research, and health care.

27. Business & Industry News. Current coverage. Cleveland, OH: Predicasts. (Vendor: DIAL)

> Updated daily, the file contains citations from articles in newspapers, business magazines, trade journals, government reports, news releases, and special reports. At the end of the week, they are transferred to the appropriate Predicast business database.

28. Business Dateline. 1985–. Louisville, KY: Data Courier. (Vendor: DIAL, VU)

> A full-text database for regional business activities and trends taken from over a hundred regional publications.

29. D&B–Dun's Market Identifiers. Current coverage. Parsippany, NJ: Dun's Marketing Services. (Vendor: DIAL)

> A directory file of 5,000,000 public and private companies with ten or more employees, with a net worth of $500,000 or more that includes the address, type of business, SIC number, sales, and year started.

30. D&B–Million Dollar Directory. Current coverage. Parsippany, NJ: Dun's Marketing Services. (Vendor: DIAL)

> This directory file has the address, brief financial and marketing information, and the officers of over 110,000 companies with a net worth of $500,000 or more. Also searchable by SIC number.

31. Federal and State Business Assistance. Current coverage. Springfield, VA: National Technical Information Service. (Vendor: BRS)

> The business assistance listed in this database includes technical and procurement leads, information management, marketing leads, and financial information. Each entry gives a summary of the service offered, a telephone number, address, and eligibility requirements.

32. GPO Monthly Catalog. 1976–. Washington, DC: U.S. Government Printing Office. (Vendors: BRS, DIAL)

> This is a machine-readable equivalent of the printed *Monthly Catalog of United States Government Publications,* which includes publications of U.S. federal agencies and the U.S. Congress.

33. Industry Data Sources. 1979–. Belmont, CA: Information Access Co.. (Vendors: BRS, DIAL)

> Bibliographic sources covering marketing and financial data for sixty-five major industries in the U.S. are indexed, including full information for ordering from the publisher.

34. MANAGEMENT CONTENTS. 1974–. Belmont, CA: Information Access Co. (Vendors: BRS, DIAL)

> Abstracts from over 120 U.S. and international journals, proceedings, transactions, newsletters, and research reports are included in this database.

35. National Newspaper Index. 1979–. Belmont, CA: Information Access Co. (Vendors: BRS, DIAL)

> Full indexing of the *Christian Science Monitor,* the *New York Times,* and the *Wall Street Journal* and national and international stories by staff writers of the *Washington Post* and the *Los Angeles Times* are included.

36. Newsearch. Current month only. Belmont, CA: Information Access Co. (Vendors: BRS, DIAL, MEAD)

This is a daily index to more than 1,700 local, regional, and national newspapers and periodicals. The newspaper indexing is transferred monthly to the *National Newspaper Index,* other items are transferred to *Management Contents, Trade and Industry Index,* or *Legal Resource Index.*

37. PTS F&S Indexes. 1972–. Cleveland, OH: Predicasts. (Vendors: BRS, DIAL)

Information on new products, forecasts of company sales, factors influencing future sales, price changes, sales, and licensing agreements are a few of the areas covered in this index of more than 5,000 publications.

38. PTS PROMT (Predicasts Overview of Marketing and Technology). 1972–. Cleveland, OH: Predicasts. (Vendors: BRS, DIAL, VU)

Abstracts business information in newspapers, magazines, government reports, trade journals, bank letters, and special reports covering areas such as market data, trends, and new products for a wide variety of industries. Also includes *Regional Business News,* an index of journals focusing on local developments.

39. Trade and Industry Index. 1981–. Belmont, CA: Information Access Co. (Vendors: BRS, DIAL, MEAD)

An index to major trade journals, industry-related periodicals, newspapers, *PR Newswire,* and the *Area Business Database,* which indexes local and regional business publications. Some citations are abstracted, and some are complete text.

CD-ROM/Laser Disc

40. INFOTRAC. 1984–. Belmont, CA: Information Access Co.

This is a subject index to articles in over 800 business and general magazines, including the *New York Times* (sixty days) and the *Wall Street Journal* (last year) that is searched on an IBM PC.

DICTIONARIES

41. Baker, Michael J., ed. *Macmillan Dictionary of Marketing and Advertising.* New York: Nichols Publishing Co., 1984. 217 p.

This is a general reference work, and the more technical jargon associated with media and statistical marketing techniques is not included. The concise definitions, cross-references to related terms, and brief sketches of key concepts are intended for practitioners, managers in other fields, and students.

42. Hart, Norman A., and Stapleton, John. *Glossary of Marketing Terms.* 2d ed. London: William Heineman, Ltd., 1981. 206 p.

Some of the more than 2,000 terms have descriptive explanations rather than definitive ones because many marketing terms have no accepted definition. Terms from other disciplines are included based on the frequency of use in marketing operations.

43. Shapiro, Irving J. *Dictionary of Marketing Terms.* 4th ed. Totowa, NJ: Littlefield, Adams & Co., 1981. 276 p.

The more than 5,000 entries in this edition include terms from the behavioral sciences and marketing research not included in previous editions. Numerous cross-references are included.

DIRECTORIES

General Directories

44. *Dun's Consultants Directory.* Annual. Parsippany, NJ: Dun's Marketing Service, 1986. 4,038 p.

> More than 25,000 U.S. consulting firms in 200 specialties are listed alphabetically by company name. The usual directory information also includes annual sales, date company started, business description, other locations, and officers for each agency. Indexes by geographic location for headquarters, branch offices, and business specialty are included.

45. Gill, Kay, and Boyden, Donald P. *Business Organizations, Agencies, and Publications Directory.* 3d ed. Detroit, MI: Gale Research Co., 1986. 2 vols. 2,031 p.

> This directory is a guide to modern business activity and covers thirty-nine types of business organizations, agencies and programs, facilities and services, research and education, publications, and information services. The master index also includes entries from other Gale directories. *Business Organizations, Agencies and Publications Directory Supplement* provides an up-date service to the basic volumes.

46. Maclean, Janice. ed. *Consultants and Consulting Organization Directory.* 7th ed. Detroit, MI: Gale Research Co., 1985. 2 vols. 1,750 p.

> More than 10,008 consulting firms, organizations, and individuals offering business services in 120 special fields are listed. Entries include name, addresses, telephone numbers, and details on the services offered. Access is by geographic location, industries served, subject areas, and by names of individual consultants or firms. *New Consultants* is a periodical supplement that lists newly formed consulting organizations.

47. *Marketing Services Guide and AMA Membership Directory.* Chicago: American Marketing Assn., 1986.

> A listing of over a thousand marketing support services and products, this directory is arranged by business classification, such as marketing research or direct marketing. Name and address of contact person is given. The roster of AMA members give corporate affiliation.

48. O'Brien, Jacqueline Wasserman, and Wasserman, Steven R., eds. *Statistics Sources.* 10th ed. Detroit, MI: Gale Research Co., 1986. 2 vols. 2,014 p.

> Arranged by more than 20,000 subjects, primary sources of national statistical data in American publications are listed. Principal statistical sources for each country in the world are also included.

49. Weiner, Richard. *Professional's Guide to Public Relations Services.* 5th ed. New York: Public Relations Publishing Co., Inc., 1985. 532 p.

> Companies are alphabetically arranged by services offered from communications and image consultants to mailing services, prizes, promotions, research, and telecommunications. The services offered are included in each listing.

50. *Who Knows: A Guide to Washington Experts.* Washington, DC: Washington Researchers Publishing, 1986. 440 p.

> This directory lists more than 10,000 specialists in Washington, DC who can help answer questions about industries, markets, products, or issues without charging a fee. Each is listed by name, title, address, and direct telephone number. A detailed index of 8,000 subject categories is provided.

Business Directories

51. *Dun's Business Identification Service.* Semiannual. Parsippany, NJ: Dun's Marketing Services.
>This microfiche directory of 5,000,000 companies is from the Dun's database of company credit reports. The entries are alphabetically arranged and list the address, without the zip code. No telephone numbers or other information is included.

52. *Dun's Business Rankings.* Annual. Parsippany, NJ: Dun's Marketing Services, 1986. 1,640 p.
>This ranked listing of the largest public and private companies by size within an industry, by sale, and by number of employees indicates prospects as well as competitors for the marketing manager.

53. *Dun's Census of American Business.* Annual. Parsippany, NJ: Dun's Marketing Service.
>Markets are analyzed on the national level by industry, on the state level by primary four-digit SIC categories, and on the county level by number of establishments, sales, and number of employees. These data are useful for locating consumer, retail, and industrial markets.

54. Frasca, Joanne, and Eubank, Elisabeth, eds. *National Directory of Minority-Owned Business Firms.* Annual. Lombard, IL: Business Research Services, Inc., 1986. 1,388 p.
>Compiled from over 500 federal, state, and local sources, this directory is arranged by four-digit SIC numbers. In addition to directory information, it also includes number of employees and sales when known. Also available in regional editions that include listings from the *National Directory of Women-Owned Business Firms.*

55. Frasca, Joanne, and Eubank, Elisabeth, eds. *National Directory of Women-Owned Business Firms.* Lombard, IL: Business Research Services, Inc., 1986. 1,500 p.
>Compiled from more than 500 federal, state, and local sources, this directory is arranged by four-digit SIC numbers. The usual directory information is given, and the number of employess and sales is included, if known. Also available in regional editions that include listings from the *National Directory of Minority-Owned Business Firms.*

56. *MacRae's State Industrial Directory.* Frequency varies. New York: MacRae's Industrial Directories.
>Available for most states, there are separate sections by products and services, alphabetical by company, a section by four-digit SIC codes, and a geographical section that is arranged by county and city. Includes the usual directory information and lists key personnel, number of employees, yearly gross sales ranges, year of establishment, and research facilities.

57. Marlow, Cecilia Ann, and Thomas, Robert C., eds. *The Directory of Directories.* 4th ed. Detroit, MI: Gale, Research Co., 1987. 2 vols. 1,727 p.
>Each of the directories is described and arranged in sixteen broad categories. The detailed subject index of more than 3,000 terms includes many cross-references for access to specific subjects. *Directory Information Service* is a supplement to this directory.

58. Marlow, Cecilia Ann, and Thomas, Robert C., eds. *The Directory of Directories 1987: Publishers Volume.* Detroit, MI: Gale Research Co., 1987. 775 p.

This volume is an index to the publishers whose works are listed in *The Directory of Directories.* The alphabetical listing provides addresses and telephone numbers. The geographic section is arranged by state and province and then by city.

59. *Million Dollar Directory.* Annual. Parsippany, NJ: Dun's Marketing Services. 1987. 5 vols. 9,775 p.

Approximately 160,000 public and private U.S. businesses with an indicated net worth of over $500,000 are alphabetically arranged giving officers, lines of business, SIC number, approximate sales, and number of employees. Separate industry and geographic volumes are provided.

60. *The Red Pages: Business across Indian America.* Toppenish, WA: LaCourse Communications, 1985. 282 p.

The businesses are listed by SIC number and have basic directory information. There is also a state listing by SIC numbers. The businesses included are either individually owned, owned by a tribe, or have intertribal ownership.

61. *Thomas Register of American Manufacturers and Thomas Register of Catalog Files.* New York: Thomas Publishing Co. 1986. 21 vols.

A detailed directory of products and services arranged by state, with separate volumes for an alphabetical listing of company profiles that give branch offices, asset ratings and company officials, two volumes of trademark and brand names, and an alphabetical listing of company catalogs.

62. *Try Us! National Minority Business Directory.* Annual. Minneapolis, MN: National Minority Business Campaign. 383 p.

More than 5,000 minority-owned businesses capable of national or regional sales are listed by categories and then alphabetical by states. A keyword index and an alphabetical listing of firms are included.

GUIDES TO INFORMATION SOURCES

63. Brownstone, David M., and Carruth, Gorton. *Where to Find Business Information: A Worldwide Guide for Everyone Who Needs the Answer to Business Questions.* 2d ed. New York: Wiley, 1982. 632 p.

More than 5,000 annotated sources of business information, including loose-leaf services, newsletters, trade periodicals, databases, annuals, textbooks, and government publications are indexed by subject. Title and publisher indexes are provided.

64. Daniells, Lorna M. *Business Information Sources.* rev. ed. Berkeley, CA: University of California Press, 1985. 673 p.

A comprehensive guide to sources for all types of business information that is needed by the businessperson, student, and librarian. Basic business sources, U.S. and foreign economic statistics and trends, industry statistics, sources for locating information on companies, organizations and individuals are included. Each entry has a descriptive annotation. The detailed author, title, and subject index provides access to specific topics.

65. Frank, Nathalie, D., and Ganly, John V. *Data Sources for Business and Market Analysis.* 3d ed. Metuchen, NJ: Scarecrow Press, 1983. 470 p.

An annotated guide to printed data sources available from U.S. government agencies, regional and local sources, foreign organizations, university programs, research institutions, and professional and trade associations. Periodicals, directories, abstracts, and indexes, and general research aids are also included. The detailed table of contents and index assist in locating information on a specific topic.

66. Goldstucker, Jac L., ed. and Echemendia, Otto R., comp. *Marketing Information: A Professional Reference Guide.* 2d ed. Atlanta, GA: Business Publications Division, College of Business Administration, Georgia State University, 1987. 384 p.
> The first part of this publication is an extensive directory of marketing associations, marketing research services and consulting organizations, the largest advertising agencies, special libraries and information centers, research centers, marketing education programs, and U.S. government agencies and organizations. The second part is an annotated bibliography of marketing books and periodicals that are arranged by marketing subjects and disciplines. Title, section, and publisher indexes are provided.

67. Hoel, Arline A.; Clarkson, Kenneth W.; and Roy, Leroy. *Economics Sourcebook of Government Statistics.* Lexington, MA: Lexington Books, 1983. 271 p.
> The fifty widely used, government statistical series described in this book are primarily concerned with business conditions including inflation measures, profits, financial indicators, and labor statistics. Information about the indicators includes name, issuing agency, coverage, available data, related series, source of data, limitations, primary and secondary sources, reference sources, and contact person for additional information.

68. Lavin, Michael R. *Business Information: How to Find It, How to Use It.* Phoenix, AZ: Oryx Press, 1987. 299 p.
> For the inexperienced user of business publications, this book explains not only how to find information on trademarks, corporate finances, industry statistics, and marketing advice, but also illustrates the explanations with reproductions of sample pages.

69. Mayros, Van, and Werner, D. Michael. *Information Sourcebook for Marketers and Strategic Planners.* Radnor, PA: Chilton Book Co., 1983. 326 p.
> This book focuses on strategic information sources covering marketing planning, sales planning, marketing and sales promotion, general management issues, and long-range strategic planning. Section one is a title listing by subtopics. Section two has brief annotations for each title, arranged by type of material. Detailed information about online databases is included.

70. Woy, James, ed. *Encyclopedia of Business Information Sources: A Bibliographic Guide to Approximately 22,000 Citations Covering More Than 1,100 Primary Subjects of Interest to Business Personnel.* 6th ed. Detroit, MI: Gale Research Co., 1986. 878 p.
> The subjects are arranged alphabetically, and each has a list of general works, abstracts, indexes, bibliographies, directories, encyclopedias, financial rations, handbooks, databases, periodicals, and associations. Citations to the correct or related topics are included. *Encyclopedia of Business Information Sources: Supplement* updates this publication and provides new sources of business information.

HANDBOOKS

71. Beacham, Walton; Hise, Richard T.; and Tongren, Hale N. *Beacham's Marketing Reference.* Washington, DC: Research Publications, 1986. 2 vols. 1,045 p.

An alphabetical arrangement of 265 marketing concepts each of which is explained with examples that describe benefits, implementation, and evaluation of the importance of these terms to the success of the business. The explanations are written by marketing experts in jargon-free language.

72. Bobrow, Edwin E., and Bobrow, Mark David. *Marketing Handbook.* Homewood, IL: Dow Jones Irwin, 1985. 2 vols.

Volume one, *Marketing Practices,* is a state-of-the-art handbook in applied marketing covering areas such as consumer and industrial goods and services, international marketing, product life cycle, marketing research, and developing the marketing plan. How-to applications are included to help develop new approaches to marketing. Volume two, *Marketing Management,* has chapters on the role of the manager in planning, training, selection of distribution channels, organization of a department, measurement techniques, new product development, and the legal aspects of marketing. Each volume has its own subject and name index.

73. Seltz, David D. *Handbook of Innovative Marketing Techniques.* Reading MA: Addison-Wesley, 1981. 329 p.

The practical and economical sales and marketing techniques included in this book cover sales promotion, new sales, advertising concepts, image building, administration, financing, and examples of sales and collection letters.

INDEXES

74. *Business Index.* Monthly. Belmont, CA: Information Access Company.

A microfilm index of journals and newspapers that covers business publications and business information from general and legal periodicals, the *Wall Street Journal, New York Times, Barrons.* Topics cover all aspects of marketing and company information and is updated monthly, with coverage of about three years on a reel. Microfiche copy from 1979 through 1983 is available. The *Business Collection* is a companion service that provides full-text microfilm copies of the indexed articles.

75. *Business Periodicals Index.* 11/yr. with annual cumulation. New York: H.W. Wilson.

This is the basic business index found in most college, university, and public libraries that provides a detailed subject index to about 300 selected business periodicals. An author listing of book reviews appears in the indexed periodicals at the end of each issue.

76. *Conference Board Cumulative Index.* Annual. New York: Conference Board.

A subject index to the publications of this research firm for areas of consumer research, corporate relations, economic and policy analysis, human resources, and management. Included are studies, pamphlets, and articles published in the last five years.

77. *Current Contents: Social & Behavioral Sciences.* Weekly. Philadelphia, PA: Institute for Scientific Information.

This publication reproduces tables of contents from more than 1,300 periodicals in the social and behavioral sciences, covering many aspects of business. Each issue has a subject index based on the title words of the articles. A useful publication for current awareness.

78. *New York Times Index.* Semimonthly with annual cumulation. New York: New York Times Co.

A detailed subject and name index which gives citations in chronological order. Some brief summaries are included.

79. *Predicasts F&S Index: United States.* Weekly with quarterly and annual cumulations. Cleveland, OH: Predicasts, Inc.

Over 1,000 sources, including magazines, newspapers, government reports, and other relevant business publications, are indexed in two sections. One section is by product/service, indexed by modified SIC, and the other is alphabetical by company name.

80. *Wall Street Journal Index: Barron's Index.* Monthly with annual cumulation. New York: Dow Jones. 2 vols.

The *Wall Street Journal* volume of the index has separate listings for corporate and general news. The *Barron's* volume combines corporate and general news and authors in one listing. Brief summaries in chronological order accompany the citations in both volumes.

PAPERS—COLLECTED

81. Alsop, Ronald, and Abrams, Bill. *The Wall Street Journal on Marketing.* Homewood, IL: Dow Jones-Irwin, 1986. 294 p.

This is a collection of the columns on marketing that appeared in the *Wall Street Journal* since 1980. Based on real-world examples or case studies, rather than theory, they are intended for a broad audience of marketing professionals, executives, and consumers. No index is included, but the articles are listed by broad categories in the table of contents.

82. Enis, Ben M., and Cos, Keith K., eds. *Marketing Classics: A Selection of Influential Articles.* 5th ed. Boston: Allyn and Bacon, 1985. 459 p.

A selection of works by various authorities in the fields, which are thought to have enduring significance to marketing thought and are widely quoted, are included in this collection.

83. Gumpert, David E., ed. *The Marketing Renaissance.* New York: Wiley, 1985. 578 p.

A collection of thirty-nine articles from *Harvard Business Review* that covers the development of marketing strategy during rapidly changing conditions for companies and the economy. Useful for an analytical approach rather than specifically practical.

PERIODICAL DIRECTORIES

84. Darnay, Brigitte T., and Nimchuk, John. *Newsletters Directory.* 3d ed. Detroit, MI: Gale Research Co., 1987. 1,162 p.

The more than 8,000 newsletter entries are arranged in thirty-two subject chapters. Full bibliographical information also includes descriptive information and online availability. Four indexes provide title, publisher, subject, and format (hard copy, online, etc.) information.

85. *Gale Directory of Publications: An Annual Guide to Newspapers, Magazines, Journals and Other Periodicals.* Detroit, MI: Gale Research Co., 1987. 1,453 p.
Formerly titled *Ayer Directory of Publications* and more recently *IMS Directory of Publications,* this directory includes expanded coverage of periodicals and newspapers published in the U.S. and Canada. The directory is geographically arranged by state and city and has alphabetical and classified indexes.

86. *Guide to Industry Special Issues.* Cambridge, MA: Ballinger Publishing Co., 1984. 733 p.
Special issues from a wide variety of trade and industry journals have annotated listings. Indexes provide access by industry, geographic division, SIC number, title, and subject.

87. Hagood, Patricia. *The Oxbridge Directory of Ethnic Periodicals: The Most Comprehensive Guide to U.S. & Canadian Ethnic Periodicals Available.* New York: Oxbridge Communications, 1979. 247 p.
Newspapers, magazines, journals, bulletins, directories, yearbooks, bibliographies, and association publications for more than seventy ethnic groups in North America are listed in this publication. Oxbridge Computer Services provides online access to this publication.

88. Hagood, Patricia. ed. *Standard Periodical Directory 1987.* 10th ed. New York: Oxbridge Communications, 1987. 1,660 p.
Annotated entries of more than 70,000 periodicals published in the United States and Canada are arranged by 230 major subjects. A detailed title and subject index are included.

89. *Irregular Serials & Annuals: An International Directory.* 12th ed. New York: Bowker, 1986. 1,899 p.
Worldwide in scope, more than 35,500 serials, annuals, continuations, conference proceedings, and other publications issued irregularly or less frequently than twice a year are alphabetically arranged by title, under 466 subject headings. A list of serials available online and a title index are provided.

90. *The Serials Directory: An International Reference Book.* Birmingham, AL: EBSCO Publishing, 1986. 3 vols. 4,505 p.
More than 113,000 serial titles including periodicals, annuals, and irregular serials published worldwide are listed by subject. Entries include bibliographic information, very brief contents information, and indexing for some titles. Volume three is a title index.

91. Thomas, Robert C., ed. *Encyclopedia of Associations: Association Periodicals.* Annual. Detroit, MI: Gale Research Co., 3 vols.
More than 18,000 journals, magazines, bulletins, newsletters, directories, which are published by trade associations, professional societies, and nonprofit organizations, are included in this directory. Arranged by broad subject categories, the descriptive entries include basic information. Subject, organization, name/acronym, publication, and title/keyword indexes are included. Volume one is *Business, Finance, Industry and Trade Publications.*

92. Uhland, Miriam, ed. *Guide to Special Issues and Indexes of Periodicals.* 3d ed. Washington, DC: Special Libraries Assn., 1985. 160 p.
More than 1,350 U.S. and Canadian periodical special issues including directories, buyers' guides, convention issues, statistical outlooks or reviews, or supplementary issues that are published on a continuing basis are listed alphabetically by title with complete bibliographical information. A subject index is provided.

93. *Ulrich's International Periodicals Directory: A Classified Guide to Current Periodicals, Foreign and Domestic.* 25th ed. New York: Bowker, 1986. 2 vols. 2,272 p.

A comprehensive list of periodicals, based on the Bowker International Serials Database, lists 68,000 periodicals in 534 subject areas, limited to periodicals issued more frequently than once a year and on a regular basis. Newspaper and government publications are omitted. Title and subject indexes are provided.

PERIODICALS

94. *Journal of Macromarketing.* Semiannual. Boulder, CO: Business Research Divisions, University of Colorado.

A scholarly journal highlighting the importance of macromarketing to industrial policy and strategy. Interest is in marketing analysis applied to countries or regions, social and comparative marketing, and the role of marketing in economic development.

95. *Journal of Marketing.* Quarterly. Chicago: American Marketing Assn.

Serving as a bridge between the scholarly and practical approach, articles cover topics such as consumer behavior, business marketing, marketing theory, and strategic market planning. Interest is in new ideas or suggestions of new concepts instead of information on the present state of the art. "Marketing Literature Review" is a briefly annotated list of journal articles from the ABI/INFORM database in a classified arrangement.

96. *Journal of Marketing Education.* 3/yr. Boulder, CO: Business Research Division, University of Colorado.

This periodical is for the exchange of ideas, information, and experience related to the education of students of marketing

97. *Journal of Public Policy and Marketing.* Annual. Ann Arbor, MI: Graduate School of Business Administration, University of Michigan.

Journal articles present empirical and theoretical research on the impact of public policy on marketing practices and the application of marketing research on public policy issues.

98. *Journal of the Academy of Marketing Science.* Quarterly. Coral Gables, FL: Academy of Marketing Science, School of Business Administration, University of Miami.

A scholarly journal that includes research articles on areas such as buyer behavior, retailing, wholesaling, marketing management, research and forecasting, channels of distribution, pricing, sales management, and industrial marketing.

99. *Marketing Communications.* Monthly. New York: Media Horizons, Inc.

Feature articles cover marketing planning and strategies, advertising, media, retailing, telemarketing, and direct marketing. Surveys such as *Product Profile Fact Book, Advertising and Promotional Expenditures,* and *Marketing Services Yearbook* are included in special issues.

100. *Marketing Intelligence and Planning.* Quarterly. Bradford, West Yorkshire, England: MCB University Press.

Aimed at the marketing practitioner, the emphasis is on the contribution of marketing research to company profit. Information on topics such as advertising effectiveness, marketing information systems, technological forecasting, uses of concept marketing, and test marketing are included.

101. *Marketing News.* Biweekly. Chicago: American Marketing Assn.
This newspaper covers what's new in marketing with articles written by staff and marketing professionals, both educators and business people. Several special issues each year cover topics such as marketing research, technology for marketing, and marketing education.

102. *Marketing Science.* Quarterly. Providence, RI: Institute of Management Science and Operations Society of America.
A scholarly journal that publishes quantitatively oriented marketing papers on theory development, marketing models, measurement, and applications. Also included are reviews of the latest trends in disciplines of interest to marketing—behavioral choice models, economic choice models, and decision analysis. State-of-the-art academic papers on key issues of current interest in marketing are also published.

103. *Marketing Times: Update for the Sales Management and Marketing Professional.* Quarterly. Cleveland, OH: Sales & Marketing Executives.
A professional/educational journal covering pertinent topics in marketing and sales aimed at the marketing executive.

104. *Marketing Update: Weekly Review of Innovative Marketing, Sales and Communication Ideas for Professional Marketers.* Weekly. Cleveland, OH: Predicasts, Inc.
Brief annotations of articles from business journals and newspapers report new ideas and strategies concerning market data and trends, growth opportunities, market research and testing, product management, and channels of distribution.

105. *Psychology and Marketing.* Quarterly. New York: Wiley.
The title indicates the focus of the articles which is the application of psychological theories and techniques to marketing interest such as buyer behavior, marketing research, and organizational development and behavior including case studies and cross-cultural aspects.

106. *The Quarterly Review of Marketing.* Quarterly. Berks, England: Institute of Marketing, Moor Hall, Cookham, Maidenhead, Berkshire.
A scholarly journal of original and recent papers covering all aspects of marketing.

PROCEEDINGS

107. AMA Winter Educator's Conference. *Marketing Education, Knowledge, Development, Dissemination and Utilization.* Chicago: American Marketing Assn., 1986. 229 p.
The papers of marketing educators cover the development, assessment, dissemination, and utilization of marketing knowledge, the impact of computing and telecommunications on marketing as a discipline, personal selling, and sales and retail management.

108. Anderson, Paul, and Ryan, Michael J., eds. *Scientific Methods in Marketing.* Chicago: American Marketing Assn., 1984. 299 p.
Papers presented at this conference cover approaches to science; theory development; social issues; channels of distribution; organizational, individual, and personal consumption; marketing management; and empirical methods.

109. Bagozzi, Richard P., et al., eds. *Marketing in the 80's: Changes and Challenges.* Chicago: American Marketing Assn., 1980. 538 p.
Focus of the papers from this conference is on the problems and opportunities for marketing in this decade covering topics such as marketing education, consumers, personal selling, segmentation, management, strategic marketing, survey research, and special markets.

110. Bush, Ronald F., and Hunt, Shelby D., eds. *Marketing Theory, Philosophy of Science Perspectives.* Chicago: American Marketing Assn., 1982. 315 p.
This special conference on marketing theory provided a forum for presentation and discusion of theoretical rather than empirical papers to assist in developing theoretical constructs capable of generating hypotheses to be tested.

111. Crawford, John C., and Garland, Barbara C., eds. *Southwestern Marketing Association Conference Proceedings.* Chicago: The Association, 1985. 263 p.
Papers presented at this conference cover topics such as buyer behavior, marketing communication, marketing research, management and strategy, marketing theory and education, distribution, and retailing.

112. *Developments in Marketing Science.* Annual. Coral Gables, FL: Academy of Marketing Science, School of Business Administration, University of Miami.
This publicaiton is a collection of papers presented at the annual conference of the Academy of Marketing Science. Contemporary marketing topics such as consumer behavior, business marketing, marketing management, marketing of services, and research methods are some areas covered.

113. *From Advertising to Communication Research: How Research Can Help Companies and Other Organizations to Communicate Effectively Both Internally and to the Outside World.* Chicago: American Marketing Assn., 1981. 376 p.
This book includes the papers presented at the second conference sponsored by the American Marketing Association and the European Society for Opinion and Marketing Research. Product/brand/service advertising, the corporate image, and internal communication are the broad categories for the papers.

114. Lamb, Charles W., Jr., and Dunne, Patrick M. *Theoretical Developments in Marketing.* Chicago: American Marketing Assn., 1980. 269 p.
The papers from this conference cover the theory of pricing, physical distribution, marketing research, channel behavior, exchange and marketing, macromarketing, and consumer behavior.

115. Lumpkin, James R., and Crawford, John C. *Southwestern Marketing Association Conference Proceedings.* Chicago: The Association, 1984. 262 p.
Some of the topics covered in these papers include approaches to marketing education, issues in mass communication, distribution issues, demographic patterns and buyer behavior, theoretical issues in marketing and research methods, and health care and nonprofit marketing.

116. Walker, Bruce J., et al., eds. *An Assessment of Marketing Thought & Practice.* Chicago: American Marketing Assn., 1982. 465 p.
A collection of papers presented at an Educators' Conference that discussed marketing issues, concepts, techniques and trends of buyer behavior, marketing education, marketing strategy, and research methodology.

ASSOCIATIONS—DIRECTORIES

117. *Directory of Business, Trade and Public Policy Organizations.* Washington, DC: Small Business Administration, U.S. Government Printing Office, 1982. 134 p.

More than 1,000 trade and business organizations are arranged by industry including some state and regional business organizations and public policy groups.

118. Gruber, Katherine. Annual. *Encyclopedia of Associations.* Detroit, MI: Gale Resarch Co. 4 vols.

Volume one, in two parts, is a comprehensive listing of national organizations classified by broad categories with seventeen points of information for each entry. Part three is the expanded *Name and Key Word Index* which also lists consultants, research, and information centers in other Gale reference publications. Volume two is a geographic and executive index. Volume three, *New Associations and Projects,* supplies information on new organizations. Volume four lists nonprofit organizations with international memberships.

119. *National Trade and Professional Associations of the United States and Canada and Labor Unions.* Annual. Washington, DC: Columbia Books, Inc.

More than 6,000 associations and labor unions are arranged alphabetically in this annual directory. In addition, to basic information, publications, meeting dates, historical notes, and brief budget information is included. Separate subject, geographic, budget, acronym, and association management companies indexes are provided.

ASSOCIATIONS

American Marketing Association. 250 W. Wacker Dr., Suite 200, Chicago, IL 60606.

Institute of Advanced Marketing Studies. 429 Lexington Ave., New York, NY 10017.

Marketing Communications Executives International. 1831 Chestnut St., Philadelphia, PA 19103.

Marketing Education Association. 1908 Association Dr., Reston, VA 22091.

Marketing Science Institute. 1000 Massachusetts Ave., Cambridge, MA 02138.

Midwest Marketing Association. c/o Carol Anderson, Marketing Department, Southern Illinois University, Carbondale, IL 62201.

Sales and Marketing Executives International. 6151 Wilson Mills Rd., Suite 200, Cleveland, OH 44143.

Southern Marketing Association. c/o John R. Brooks, Executive Secretary, College of Business and Technology, West Texas State University, Canyon, TX 79016.

Southwestern Marketing Association. c/o Bob Leone, President, Department of Marketing, The University of Texas at Austin, Austin, TX 78712.

Marketing Management

BIBLIOGRAPHIES

120. Fildes, Robert Dews, and David, Howell Syd. *A Bibliography of Business and Economic Forecasting.* New York: Facts on File, 1981. 424 p.
Journal articles from thirty journals and books published from 1971 to 1978, and a few important earlier references are included in this bibliography. The citations are indexed by some 500 topics for quick access to a specific subject. Some articles are labeled as basic or advanced to indicate the level of mathematical complexity. Material is useful for the manager, student, or academician.

BUSINESS/SALES FORECASTING

121. Hurwood, David L.; Grossman, Elliott S.; and Bailey, Earl L. *Sales Forecasting.* New York: Conference Board, 1978. 226 p.
A study by the Conference Board which provides information on sales forecasting practices that show the practical working of various forecasting methods and how companies solve their forecasting problems. Covered are areas such as judgmental forecasting, sales force estimation, various techniques and methods, and new product and long-term sales forecasting.

122. Kress, George. *Practical Techniques of Business Forecasting: Fundamentals and Applications for Marketing, Productions and Financial Management.* Westport, CT: Quorum Books, Greenwood Press, 1985. 257 p.
The basic information in this book helps the marketing manager interpret and use forecasts for making decisions. Underlying assumptions are explained in understandable language with step-by-step guidance through the techniques, limiting information to what an executive should know about complex processes.

123. Marino, Kenneth E. *Forecasting Sales and Planning Profits: A No-Nonsense Guide for the Growing Business.* Chicago: Probus Publishing Co., 1986. 177 p.
This book explains and illustrates the steps involved in forecasting sales and revenues that are based on the market potential/sales requirement method. The result is a cost-effective and reliable approach for management.

124. Rao, Vithala R., and Cox, James E., Jr. *Sales Forecasting Methods: A Survey of Recent Developments.* Cambridge, MA: Marketing Science Institute, 1978. 167 p.
Aimed at the business and academic researcher, this literature review consists of a summary, a comparison and critique of models and methods used in sales forecasting. A semiannotated bibliography of articles and books is also provided.

125. White, Harry R. *Sales Forecasting: Timesaving and Profit-Making Strategies That Work.* Glenview, IL: Scott, Foresman & Co., 1984. 180 p.
This book reviews the basics and presents ways to improve a company's forecasting methods. Topics discussed include sales force estimates, using Time-Series analysis, forecasting with econometrics, new product forecasting, and use of the computer.

COMPUTER SOFTWARE DIRECTORIES

126. *Datapro Directory of Software.* Loose-leaf with periodic updates. Delran, NJ: Datapro Research Corp. 3 vols.
An up-to-date service that provides descriptive information and user ratings of available software for a wide variety of business applications. Indexes by applications, product names, vendor/product, and hardware provide several ways to identify software for a specific need.

127. *The Software Catalog: Microcomputers.* Quarterly. New York: Elsevier. 3 vols.
The more than 22,000 software programs, arranged alphabetically by more than 400 vendor names, are listed in part one and two. Part three has the indexes for systems, including computer, operating and program languages, subject and application, keyword, and program name. Each entry gives availability, price, applications, and compatibility of the software package.

128. *The Software Catalog: Minicomputers.* Semiannual. New York: Elsevier.
Descriptions of over 7,800 programs are provided. The main criterion for inclusion in this list is the cost of the computer system on which the program will run. There is some lapover with programs in both the microcomputer and minicomputer listings. Information on availability, price, applications, and compatibility is included.

DATABASES

129. Business Software Database. Current coverage. Berkeley, CA: Information Sources, Inc. (Vendor: BRS)
Descriptions of software products for mini- and microcomputers include availability, hardware and operating system compatibility, price, documentation, and customer support provided.

130. Business Software Database. Current coverage. Louisville, KY: Data Courier, Inc. (Vendor: DIAL)
Descriptive information for business software packages for micro- and minicomputers includes program languages, compatible hardware and operating systems, vendor, contact person, price information, and the number of installations.

131. Commerce Business Daily. 1982–. Washington, DC: U.S. Government Printing Office. (Vendor: DIAL)
The full text of this daily publication, which announces products and services needed by the U.S. government, is searchable online.

132. D&B–Dun's Electronic Yellow Pages. Current coverage. Mountain Lakes, NJ: Donnelley Marketing Services. (Vendor: DIAL)
These databases have company and individual listings from telephone and state directories, state industrial listings, and special directories. The Electronic Yellow Pages Index database is by SIC number and is used to determine which directory to search.

D&B-Dun's Electronic Yellow Pages–Financial Services Directory.
D&B-Dun's Electronic Yellow Pages–Manufacturers Directory.
D&B-Dun's Electronic Yellow Pages–Professionals Directory.
D&B-Dun's Electronic Yellow Pages–Retailers Directory.
D&B-Dun's Electronic Yellow Pages–Services Directory.
D&B-Dun's Electronic Yellow Pages–Wholesalers Directory.
Electronic Yellow Pages Index.

133. Thomas Register. Current coverage. Thomas Publishing Co., Inc. (Vendor: DIAL)

A product directory of American industry that includes more than 50,000 different classes of products from 134,000 manufacturers.

GUIDEBOOKS/HANDBOOKS

134. Aaker, David A. *Strategic Market Management.* New York: Wiley, 1984. 336 p.

Based on a comprehensive flow model, strategic market management involves external analysis of customers, competitors, industry and environment, and self-analysis. The emphasis is on the externally proactive approach.

135. Ames, B. Charles, and Hlavacek, James D. *Managerial Marketing: The Ultimate Advantage.* Mountainside, NJ: Managerial Marketing, Inc., 1984. 389 p.

A how-to book that focuses on the need for management to make marketing a powerful force in a company. It deals with practical business concepts and proven principles and illustrates them with real-life situations, covering market evaluation, marketing mix, developing and evaluating plans, and managing the organization.

136. Bencin, Richard L. *The Marketing Revolution: Understanding Major Changes in How Businesses Market.* Philadelphia, PA: Swansea Press, Inc., 1984. 219 p.

The "new marketing" includes major changes in the way products are marketed, and some factors causing the changes include global competition, maturing of industries, deregulation, computerization, breakup of the mass market, and sales costs increases. The use of technology, direct marketing, and scientific marketing are detailed to indicate trends.

137. Bonoma, Thomas V. *The Marketing Edge: Making Strategies Work.* New York: Free Press, 1985. 241 p.

This book covers marketing practices, and some factors that help marketers manage marketing structures and provides guides to the execution of plans, programs, and strategies. Monitoring and organizing programs and systems, interacting and allocating skills are some areas included.

138. Bradway, Bruce M.; Frenzel, Mary Anne; and Pritchard, Robert E. *Strategic Marketing: A Handbook for Entrepreneurs and Managers.* Reading MA: Addison-Wesley, 1982. 238 p.

The basic elements of strategic market planning are covered in this practical guide which will assist owners and managers in applying planning disciplines to their business.

139. Britt, Steuart Henderson, and Guess, Norman F., eds. *Dartnell Marketing Manager's Handbook.* 2d ed. Chicago: Dartnell Corp., 1983. 1,293 p.

The most effective marketing principles for developing a marketing plan that meets the competition and provides for long range planning, but one that is flexible for adjustment to constantly changing marketing conditions are covered. Partial contents include organizing and staffing, establishing marketing objectives, and putting the marketing plan into action.

140. Buell, Victor P., ed. *Handbook of Modern Marketing.* 2d ed. New York: McGraw-Hill, 1986. 1,296 p.

Designed for marketing managers at all levels, each chapter is written by an expert in the field. A practical treatment of the major markets—consumer, industrial, service, and government—can be understood by the generalist. In addition to basic subjects, areas such as non-business marketing, corporate identification, using market consultants, marketing control systems, and automatic retailing are included.

141. Chase, Cochrane, et al. *Solving Marketing Problems with VisiCalc.* Radnor, PA: Chilton Book Co., 1984. 286 p.

Not designed to replace basic instructions, the book assumes basic familiarity with this software. The step-by-step instructions cover areas such as product planning, pricing, revenue scheduling, competitive bidding, distribution and sales, advertising, direct mail, and marketing research.

142. Cohen, William A. *Winning on the Marketing Front: The Corporate Manager's Game Plan.* New York: Wiley, 1986. 381 p.

Planning and strategy are the keys to business success, and this book explains the basic concept of strategy as developed by academic and military theorists. Use of the planning forms provide aid in solving strategic problems and developing winning strategies.

143. Davis, Robert T., and Smith, F. Gordon. *Marketing in Emerging Companies.* Reading, MA: Addison-Wesley, 1984. 159 p.

For the management of a new company, this book provides practical advice on the marketing plan, marketing strategy, the dynamics of market strategy, selling, and sales management. Three important considerations are the viability of the product and the market, the capability of the company, and whether the payoff will be worthwhile.

144. Deran, Elisabeth. *Low Cost Marketing Strategies: Field-Tested Techniques for Tight Budgets.* New York: Praeger, 1987. 151 p.

For the company with a limited budget, this guide not only discusses what might be done, but also shows how to effectively promote a product. Included are techniques for getting free publicity, using telemarketing and direct marketing, matching salespeople with product type, and conducting marketing research. Sample telephone scripts, news releases, and sales letters are provided.

145. Fogg, C. Davis. *Diagnostic Marketing: Finding and Fixing Critical Problems.* Reading, MA: Addison-Wesley, 1985. 285 p.

Diagnostic marketing principles are applied to the planning, executing, and controlling of the market function. These principles include identification of the symptoms of market problems, diagnosing what is wrong with the organization, and developing intelligent, simple solutions to the problems. This is a systemtic process that can solve critical marketing problems.

146. Foxall, Gordon. *Marketing Behaviour: Issues in Managerial and Buyer Decision-Making.* Farnborough, England: Gower, 1981. 186 p.
The theoretical and applied dimensions of behavioral sciences are applied to marketing. Consumer behavior is analyzed as well as managerial decision making.

147. Goldman, Jordan. *Public Relations in the Marketing Mix: Introducing Vulnerability Relations.* Chicago: Crain Books, 1984. 165 p.
Proactive public relations reflect the company's marketing objectives, sales goals, and positioning. Reactive public relations are used to combat negative publicity about a company. Methods and techniques for both types of public relations are covered.

148. Hennessey, Hubert D. *How to Write a Marketing Plan.* rev. ed. Saranac Lake, NY: American Management Association Extension Institute, 1986. 176 p.
A self-study course that shows how to analyze the competition, set measurable goals and objectives, develop marketing strategies, forecast potential sales and market shares, build action plans, and monitor and control procedures.

149. Laric, Michael V., and Stiff, Ronald. *Multiplan for Marketing and Sales.* Englewood Cliffs, NJ: Prentice-Hall, 1984. 314 p.
Using spreadsheets in general and Multiplan in particular, this book provides ideas for solving marketing and sales problems using a personal computer. Concepts of spreadsheet models are discussed, and specific use is demonstrated for sales forecasting, cost analysis and pricing, promotions, resources, and retailing analysis.

150. Lillien, Gary L., and Kotler, Philip. *Marketing Decision Making: A Model-Building Approach.* New York: Harper & Row, 1983. 875 p.
This book is designed as a general reference for practitioners and for students. It covers major tools for building, estimating, and using quantitative marketing models. Some of the models included are micromarketing, pricing, distribution, advertising, sales promotion, sales force, market planning, and sales models for new products.

151. MacDonald, Charles R. *24 Ways to Greater Business Productivity: Master Checklist for Marketing, Advertising, Sales, Distribution, and Customer Service.* Englewood Cliffs, NJ: Institute for Business Planning, 1982. 446 p.
The detailed checklists and instructions are designed for the marketing manager who wants to improve performance of marketing functions. Self-audits provide a means of rating each function, interpreting the rating, and deciding what to do next. Some areas covered include new product planning and development, market research and analysis, and advertising.

152. Makens, James C. *The Marketing Plan Workbook.* Englewood Cliffs, NJ: Prentice-Hall, 1985. 204 p.
A practical planning book that has ready-to-use forms, tables, and worksheets that assist in organizing everything involved in market planning. Practical guidance is supplied for handling each step of the plan, and suggestions for avoiding potential problem areas are included.

153. Mayros, Van, and Werner, D. Michael. *Marketing Information Systems: Design and Applications for Marketers.* Radnor, PA: Chilton Book Co., 1982. 330 p.
Both theory and applications show the marketing professional how to examine a task and solve marketing problems. Information is presented in four sections—Design, Development, Application, and Enhancement. The marketing information system guidelines can be used as a model in any business organization.

154. McCann, John M. *The Marketing Workbench: Using Computers for Better Performance.* Homewood, IL: Dow Jones-Irwin, 1986.
The marketing workbench is a workstation for marketing managers that contains a database of most of the information needed to devise marketing strategies and programs. Areas covered include the computing environment today, future technological development and how it can be used to support marketing and sales, and an in-depth discussion of the use of the marketing workbench.

155. McDonald, Malcolm. *Marketing Plans: How to Prepare Them, How to Use Them.* New York: Franklin Watts, 1985. 216 p.
A systematic guidebook that assists managers in defining and achieving business objectives by using a series of logical activities. This is a combination of theory and practice that progresses from how planning works to setting market objectives and strategies, scheduling, costing out programs, and implementing a simple market planning system.

156. McKenna, Regis. *The Regis Touch: Million-Dollar Advice from America's Top Marketing Consultant.* Reading, MA: Addison-Wesley, 1985. 179 p.
Dynamic positioning is necessary in today's competitive world, and the key ideas are that marketing is dynamic not static, should focus on market creation not market share, and should be a building process not a promotional process. These ideas cover product, market, and corporate positioning and developing a strategy.

157. Michman, Ronald D. *Marketing to Changing Consumer Markets: Environmental Scanning.* New York: Praeger, 1983. 168 p.
Future planning is based on trends involving demographic, economic, social and cultural, political and legal, technological, ecological, and competitive forces. These changes are important for developing market strategies. By monitoring external forces, events, and relationships, an organization can develop a more successful marketing plan.

158. Morse, Stephen. *Management Skills in Marketing.* London: McGraw-Hill Book Co., Ltd., 1982. 150 p.
The skills needed by marketing managers are the focus of this book. Creative and strategic decision making is important, but getting things done is more important. This involves skills in planning, organizing, and controlling marketing, including marketing research, assessing the ingredients of the marketing mix, managing time, and communications and profit responsibility.

159. Mossman, Frank H.; Criss, W. J. E.; and Fischer, Paul M. *Financial Dimensions of Marketing Management.* New York: Wiley, 1978. 170 p.
For the manager concerned with profitability, this is a guide for refining policies and procedures that lead to profitable opportunities. The approach is based on contribution theory rather than on full-cost allocation, using a modular database. Various financial tools are also presented.

160. Myers, James H., and Tauber, Edward. *Market Structure Analysis.* Chicago: American Marketing Assn., 1977. 159 p.
The useful multivariate statistical techniques that have found application to marketing are described in this book which market planners will find helpful. Some of these techniques include multidimensional scaling methods, factor analysis, and discriminant analysis for positioning and multivariate analysis for market segmentation. A behavioral market structure model is also included.

161. Myers, John G.; Massy, William F.; and Greyser, Stephen A. *Marketing Research and Knowledge Development: An Assessment for Marketing Management.* Englewood Cliffs, NJ: Prentice-Hall, 1980. 306 p.

This is a descriptive account that deals with the nature of marketing research and the development of marketing knowledge in the U.S. over the last twenty-five years. The nature and scope of the current marketing research and development systems, presentation of various models and conceptual framework, and the impact of this research on marketing management practice are some of the areas covered.

162. Prince, Melvin. *Consumer Research for Management Decisions.* New York: Wiley, 1982. 210 p.

A practical guide for business problem solving, this book emphasizes quantitative research rather than qualitative research. It provides information, training, updating, and review so that consumer researchers can apply research methodology to solving problems in marketing strategy, product, and promotion research.

163. Schultz, Randall L., and Zoltners, Andris A. *Marketing Decision Models.* New York: Elsevier North-Holland, 1981. 298 p.

Marketing decision models developed in the last twenty years are covered. Included are descriptive models, normative marketing models, new product models, marketing-oriented strategic planning models, and market models in public and nonprofit organizations.

164. Stapleton, John. *How to Prepare a Marketing Plan.* 3d ed. Aldershot, Hampshire, England: Gower Publishing Co., Ltd., 1982. 299 p.

This book provides planning procedures based on a positive awareness of customers' needs and includes a full range of charts and diagrams. Each chapter has an explanation of a step in the process of developing a marketing plan, including the appropriate charts and diagrams to document the plan. Some of the areas covered are formulating objectives, market share analysis, new product introduction, media evaluation, budgeting, brand management, and personnel organization.

165. Stevens, Robert E. *Strategic Marketing Plan Master Guide.* Englewood Cliffs, NJ: Prentice-Hall, 1982. 209 p.

A systemic approach to strategic market planning is presented for the marketing professional. The practical orientation of the book emphasizes techniques and tools rather than theory and what the plan should contain and how to prepare it.

166. Taylor, James W. *Competitive Marketing Strategies.* Radnor, PA: Chilton Book Co., 1986. 184 p.

A step-by-step plan to develop and execute profitable market strategy that covers areas such as product life cycle, measuring and analyzing market share and competitive advantage, cost and prices, refining marketing strategies, and measuring progress.

167. Weinrauch, J. Donald. *The Marketing Problem Solver.* New York: Wiley, 1987. 319 p.

Solutions for problems in areas such as advertising and promotion, direct response marketing, research, pricing, product planning, distribution, and budgeting are provided. These solutions cover basics and help develop creative thinking to focus on the marketplace, products, and services offered by a company.

168. Wilson, Aubry. *Aubrey Wilson's Marketing Audit Check Lists.* London: McGraw-Hill Book Co., Ltd., 1982. 215 p.

These checklists provide a short cut to assembling information and avoid omitting issues or questions. A list of questions for each area, such as marketing strategy and planning or product/service range, provides the information needed for a series of basic actions.

169. Yip, George W. *The Role of Strategic Planning in Consumer- Marketing Businesses.* Cambridge, MA: Marketing Science Institute, 1984. 48 p.

The reason consumer marketing companies have not adopted strategic planning are the underlying characteristics of companies and their markets. Focusing on the characteristics of strategic planning, the author shows how to design planning systems to cope with company issues. Areas covered include a structural model of strategic planning, empirical research, and PIMS data.

PAPERS—COLLECTED

170. Laczniak, Gene R., and Murphy, Patrick E., eds. *Marketing Ethics: Guidelines for Managers.* Lexington, MA: Lexington Books, 1985. 182 p.

Intended for the manager interested in ethical issues, this collection of papers discusses the problem of marketing ethics, a framework for analyzing marketing ethics, ethical issues in marketing research, advertising, price fixing, sales management, and how to incorporate these ethics into an organization. Each paper ends with specific guidelines for management. Reprints of several organization's code of ethics are included.

171. Zoltners, Andris A., ed. *Marketing Planning Models.* New York: North-Holland Publishing Co., 1982. 276 p.

This collection of scholarly papers indicates the state-of-the-art of marketing model-building. They represent the diversity of marketing modeling applications and approaches and the difficulty in modeling marketing behavior.

PERIODICALS

172. *Journal of Business Forecasting and Systems.* Quarterly. Flushing, NY: Graceway Publishing Co.

Articles on forecasting cover a variety of topics from new product distribution, forecasting in industries, and setting up a forecasting process. The tabular presentations and interpretations of forecasts of financial institutions are included.

173. *Journal of Forecasting.* Quarterly. New York: Wiley.

A scholarly journal covering all areas of forecasting including new products, technology, production, and finances. The articles may be methodology evaluation or practical applications to business or government.

174. *Management Briefing: Marketing.* Bimonthly. New York: The Conference Board.

A newsletter that is a bimonthly briefing on current developments affecting marketing, including topics such as sales careers, new product development, technology, and consumers.

175. *Potentials in Marketing.* 9/yr. Minneapolis, MN: Lakewood Publications, Inc.

Trends in marketing, sales ideas and promotions, advertising, and management techniques are covered. Conference reports, information on training programs, and incentive plans are also included.

PROCEEDINGS

176. LaPlaca, Peter J., and Frank, Newton. *Marketing Strategies for a Tough Environment.* Chicago: American Marketing Assn., 1980. 211 p.

The papers presented at this conference cover five broad areas of government regulations, communications as a changing way of reaching markets, the impact of energy on marketing decisions, R&D, and strategic planning. Several papers are on topics associated with marketing education.

177. Thomas, Howard, and Gardner, David., eds. *Strategic Marketing and Management.* New York: Wiley, 1985. 509 p.

This is a collection of papers presented at a conference cosponsored by the Marketing Education Division of the American Marketing Association and the Department of Business Administration, University of Illinois at Urbana-Champaign. Concepts of planning, planning techniques, and their role in strategic inquiry, competitive strategy, and competition are covered.

SMALL BUSINESS

Bibliographies

178. Brannen, William H. *Small Business Marketing: A Selected and Annotated Bibliography.* Chicago: American Marketing Assn., 1978. 79 p.

Although the material is older, more than 200 references published before 1978 include citations to books, journal articles, and public documents. Some topics are product, place, prices, promotion strategies, research, and marketing

179. Ryans, Cynthia C. *Small Business: An Information Sourcebook.* Phoenix, AZ: Oryx Press, 1987. 286 p.

For the small business, this annotated bibliography covers all aspects of starting and operating a business, including chapters on advertising, public relations, franchising, marketing, sales, and strategic planning.

Guidebooks/Handbooks

180. Bolt, Gordon J. *Market and Sales Forecasting Manual.* 2d ed. Englewood Cliffs, NJ: Prentice-Hall, 1982. 335 p.

Aimed at the marketing executive of a small- to medium-sized company, this practical guide to sales forecasting examines statistical, nonstatistical, behavioral, subjective, and objective approaches in relation to the market environment and marketing influences. The part-time forecaster in a company will also find this useful.

181. Carlson, Linda. *The Publicity and Promotion Handbook: A Complete Guide for Small Business.* Boston: CBI Publishing Co., 1982. 272 p.
A guide for small business owners on how to effectively promote their business, products, and services. Techniques for producing sales brochures, press releases, and feature articles are some of the areas covered.

182. Cohen, William A., and Reddick, Marshall E. *Successful Marketing for Small Business.* New York: AMACOM, 1981. 121 p.
The practical explanations of marketing theory include techniques and processes that are important for developing a profitable marketing plan.

183. Davidson, Jeffrey P. *Marketing to the Fortune 500 and Other Corporations.* Homewood, IL: Dow Jones-Irwin, 1987. 291 p.
Inside tips that will help a small business selling products or services obtain contracts with large corporations, including a detailed plan for securing these contracts. Lists of purchasing offices, regional purchasing magazines, market research information sources, and state-sponsored support organizations are also provided.

184. Dorff, Ralph L. *Marketing for the Small Manufacturer: How to Turn the Disadvantage of Being Small into Big Business Advantage.* Englewood Cliffs, NJ: Prentice-Hall, 1983. 193 p.
Practical advice on the marketing function for the small business covers structuring of the organization, the cost benefit of marketing programs over diffused sales efforts, contacts needed for successful marketing, analyzing the product line in terms of buyer motivation, planning production through marketing forecasts, effective use of advertising, and motivating the sales agents.

185. Elster, Robert J., ed. *Small Business Sourcebook.* Detroit, MI: Gale Research, 1987. 2 vols. 1,837 p.
Key information sources for 140 specific businesses, include names of associations, franchises, supply sources, statistical sources, periodicals, consultants, and financial services. The *Small Business Sourcebook: Supplement* is an update service for the basic volumes.

186. Fenno, Brooks. *Helping Your Business Grow: 101 Dynamic Ideas in Marketing.* New York: AMACOM, 1982. 225 p.
For the small business manager, the successful marketing strategies and techniques include topics such as market planning; the art of selling; managing sales territories; finding, hiring, and training sales personnel; internal diversification; and how to fund growth.

187. Kuswa, Webster. *Big Paybacks from Small Budget Advertising.* Chicago: Dartnell Corp., 1982. 350 p.
For the small company with a limited advertising budget, this publication includes practical advice on market research and how to get free information, examples of good advertising copy, how to test copy, physical production steps, and where to place the ad.

188. Lace, Geoffrey. *Effective Marketing for the Smaller Business: A Practical Guide.* Newbury, Berkshire, England: Scope Books, Ltd., 1982. 221 p.
The marketing mix covered in this guide includes market research, sales and distribution, advertising, sales promotion, and product policy. Checklists are provided to assist in effective market planning.

189. Lemmon, Wayne A. *The Owner's and Manager's Market Analysis Workbook for Small to Moderate Retail and Service Establishments.* New York: AMACOM, 1980. 230 p.

The techniques covered in this workbook provide information for owners and managers that enables them to perform basic market analysis and to determine the potential profitability of a business in a specific location. Defining the market, estimating market size, support for the type of business, and interpretation and evaluation of calculations are some of the areas covered.

190. Levinson, Jay Conrad. *Guerrilla Marketing: Secrets for Making Big Profits from Small Business.* Boston: Houghton Mifflin Co., 1984. 226 p.

The emphasis in this book is to concentrate on simplifying the complexities in developing a marketing plan that is creative and saves money. Using minimedia techniques, such as the telephone, brochures, and the yellow pages, or maximedia consisting in part of newpapers, radio, and direct mail, or nonmedia, such as free seminars, trade shows, and T-shirts, the small entrepreneur can produce profitable results.

191. Lindberg, Roy A., and Cohn, Theodore. *The Marketing Book for Growing Companies That Want to Excel.* New York: Van Nostrand, 1986. 226 p.

This book is a guide to marketing thinking and decision making rather than a how-to book. However, it is factual, practical, and tuned to the formal marketing needs of smaller companies. Some areas covered include getting started, determining information needs, using information, specific strategies, planning tools, writing the plan, controlling results, and implementing the plan.

192. Marino, Kenneth E. *Forecasting Sales and Planning Profits: A No-Nonsense Guide for the Growing Business.* Chicago: Probus Publishing, 1986. 177 p.

Forecasting sales and revenues is an inexact science, even for the large company with sophisticated computer systems. For the smaller company, this is an even greater problem. In order to simplify the process, the author recommends the market potential/sales requirement method of forecasting. This book explains and illustrates the steps involved in this method for a variety of industries.

193. McCready, Gerald B. *Marketing Tactics Master Guide for Small Business.* Englewood Cliffs, NJ: Prentice-Hall, 1982. 139 p.

Emphasis is on practical advice and methods to improve the marketing effectiveness of a small business. Goal setting, marketing research, communication skills, and performance review are stressed.

194. Phillips, Michael, and Rasberry, Salli. *Marketing without Advertising: Creative Strategies for Small Business Success.* Berkeley, CA: Nolo Press, 1986. Various paging.

A practical approach to developing a low-cost marketing plan that is not based on advertising, with specific suggestions and guidance concerning business appearance, pricing, employee relations, accessibility, business practices, and use of free media access.

195. Rice, Craig S. *Marketing Planning Strategies: A Guide for Small or Medium-Sized Companies.* Chicago: Dartnell Corp., 1984. 434 p.

Successful marketing is dependent upon intelligent planning and realistic budgeting. Tested techniques and methods that are successful are presented in this practical and easy to use guide of marketing principles.

196. Smith, Roger F. *Entrepreneur's Marketing Guide.* Reston, VA: Reston Publishing Co., Inc., 1984. 239 p.

The basics of marketing are outlined for the small business entrepreneur in a practical and logical approach using real-world examples. Simple to use planning techniques cover the all-important market planning process, sales force development, advertising, and even marketing professional services.

Periodicals

197. *American Journal of Small Business.* Quarterly. Baltimore, MD: University of Baltimore.

Articles of a theoretical or practical nature are intended for academicians, consultants, government officials, and others who support the small business community.

198. *Journal of Small Business Management.* Quarterly. Morgantown, WV: Bureau of Business Research, West Virginia University.

All aspects of small business are covered in the current articles with each issue covering a specific topic.

199. *NFIB Quarterly Economic Report for Small Business.* Quarterly. San Mateo, CA: National Federation of Independent Business.

Based on a questionnaire sampling of its membership, this report supplies information on economic conditions and problems facing small business. These data include price trends, price changes, earnings trends, credit, capital expenditures, and expenses.

200. *Small Business Report: For Decision Makers in Small & Midsize Companies.* Monthly. Monterey, CA: Business Research and Communications.

Covers all aspects of small business management including topics such as sales, sales training, new product development, budgeting, sales territories, use of sales reps, and pricing decisions.

Associations

American Federation of Small Business. 407 S. Dearborn St., Chicago, IL 60605.

National Federation of Independent Business. 150 W. 20th Ave., San Mateo, CA 94403.

National Small Business Association. 1155 15th St., N.W., 7th Floor, Washington, DC 20005.

National Small Business Government Contractors Association. 405 Northfield Ave., Suite 113, West Orange, NJ 07052.

Marketing Research

BIBLIOGRAPHIES

201. Dickson, John R. *The Bibliography of Marketing Research Methods.* 2d ed. Lexington, MA: Published for the Marketing Science Institute by Lexington Books, 1986. 788 p.

> More than 9,000 entries for books, articles, handbooks, and conference proceedings are organized into the three broad categories—marketing research function, data collection methods, and data analysis techniques. These are further subdivided by many headings and subheadings for specific subjects. An author and subject index are provided.

202. Ferber, Robert, et al., comp. *A Basic Bibliography on Marketing Research.* 3d ed. Chicago: American Marketing Assn., 1974. 299 p.

> An expanded edition of an earlier publication, this annotated bibliography covers the pertinent literature of marketing research through 1973. Marketing research is broadly defined to include social sciences and other disciplines, including concepts and methods in areas which are applicable to marketing research.

203. Michman, Ronald D.; Gable, Myron; and Cross, Walter. *Market Segmentation: A Selected and Annotated Bibliography.* Chicago: American Marketing Assn., 1977. 58 p.

> Intended for scholars, students, and market practitioners, this bibliography includes books and journal articles published from 1956 to 1975. The bibliography covers conceptual foundations of segmentation, behavioral variables, purchasing influences, the role of qualitative dimensions in decision making, and the use of multivariate analysis.

DATABASES

Online

204. ASI–American Statistics Index. 1973–. Washington, DC: Congressional Information Services, Inc. (Vendor: DIAL)

> A comprehensive index of more than 500 U.S. federal statistical publications covering social, economic, and demographic data.

205. D&B–Donnelley Demographics. Annual reloads. Mountain Lakes, NJ: Donnelley Marketing Services. (Vendor: DIAL)

> Demographic data from the 1980 U.S. census as well as five-year estimates and projections provide information for all states, counties, towns, Zip code areas, Standard Metropolitan Statistical Areas, Primary Metropolitan Statistical Areas, Metropolitan Statistical Areas, and summaries for the U.S.

206. Disclosure Online. Current coverage. Bethesda, MD: Disclosure Information Group. (Vendors: BRS, DIAL, VU)

> Information on more than 11,000 companies that is derived from the reports filed with the Securities and Exchange Commission includes financial and sales information useful for marketing intelligence and corporate planning.

207. Findex: The Directory of Market Research Reports, Studies and Surveys. 1977–. Bethesda, MD: National Standards Assn. (Vendors: DIAL)

> More than 12,000 citations with abstracts, covering fifty-five industries are indexed by broad category and by specific industry or product. The listed items are commercially available from U.S. and international publishers.

208. Frost & Sullivan Research Reports. New York: Frost & Sullivan, (Vendor: BRS)

> Abstracts of reports that analyze and forecast market size and share by product and company of industries such as communications, consumer products, electronics, food, and health.

209. Industry Data Sources. 1979–. Belmont, CA: Information Access Co. (Vendors: BRS, DIAL, MEAD)

> Bibliographic sources of marketing and financial data on sixty-five major industries in the U.S., Canada, and Western Europe include market research studies, economic forecasts, statistical studies, reports, and other documents. Abstracts include complete information for ordering the report.

210. Investext: The Business Intelligence Database. 1982–. Boston: Business Research Corp. (Vendors: BRS, DIAL)

> The full text of more than 35,000 research reports, written by professional analysts, and financial and major investment banking research firms, cover some 1,000 of the largest publicly held companies and 500 smaller companies representing fifty industries. Sales, earnings, market share, and related financial data are some of the areas included.

211. PsycINFO. 1967–. Washington, DC: American Psychological Assn. (Vendors: BRS, DIAL)

> References on relevant original research in psychology and the behavioral sciences from more than 1,400 perioidcals, dissertations, technical reports, and other sources are included. Marketing, advertising, mass media, and consumer research are some areas of interest to marketers.

212. PTS U.S. Forecasts. 1971–. Cleveland, OH: Predicasts, Inc. (Vendor: DIAL)

> Includes abstracts of short- and long-range forecasts for many industries and products that are published in trade journals, business and financial publications, newspapers, government reports, and special studies.

213. TRINET Company Database. Current coverage. Parsippany, NJ: TRINET, Inc. (Vendors: DIAL, MEAD)

Current financial and marketing data are provided on U.S. single and multiestablishment, private and public, manufacturing and nonmanufacturing companies with more than twenty employees and for all product areas and sectors.

214. *TRINET Establishment Database.* Current coverage. Parsippany, NJ: TRINET, Inc. (Vendors: DIAL, MEAD)

Data on more than 400,000 private and public, manufacturing and nonmanufacturing business establishments emphasize information on branch locations, including market share.

CD-ROM/Optical Disc

215. Datext. Monthly updates. Woburn, MA: Datext, Inc.

A database on compact disc with financial and textual information on 10,000 public companies on four separate discs. The subject areas on the discs are consumers, industrial, service, and technology. The information is from six business databases, and the system selects the data from any one of these.

216. PsycLIT. Quarterly updates. Wellesly Hills, MA: Silver Platter Information.

Abstracts from more than 1,400 journals covering psychology and the behavioral sciences are included in this database. The beginning date is 1974.

DICTIONARIES

217. Dutka, Solomon, and Roshwalb, Irving. *A Dictionary for Marketing Research.* New York: Audits & Surveys, Inc., 1983. 73 p.

Selected technical words that make up the jargon of marketing research are included. Many of these terms are borrowed from other disciplines but have a different meaning when applied to marketing research. This is also true of the borrowed general usage words. Each page has two columns, one for the definition and the other for a citation to a publication that has a detailed discussion of the term.

218. van Minden, J. J. R. *Dictionary of Marketing Research.* Chicago: St. James Press, 1987. 200 p.

The terms used in marketing, marketing research, advertising, and public relations are defined and related to theory, including examples from marketing. The more than 2,000 terms are arranged in seven broad areas.

DIRECTORIES

219. *Bradford's Directory of Marketing Research Agencies and Management Consultants in the United States and the World.* Annual. Fairfax, VA: Bradford's Directory of Marketing Research Agencies.

The more than 900 agencies and consultants included in this edition are arranged alphabetically by state or country. Indexes by type of marketing research, an alphabetical listing of agencies and key personnel, and a list of associations are provided.

220. *Directory of U.S. and Canadian Marketing Surveys and Services.* 5th ed. Bridgewater, NJ: Rausch Associates, Inc., 1985. 402 p.

Marketing reports written within the last four years and services available from 275 consulting firms are alphabetically arranged by company name. The studies are divided into three sections—continuing services, individual surveys over $1,000, and individual surveys under $1,000. A detailed company specialty index and a subject index provide access to specific items or services.

221. *Findex: The Directory of Market Research Reports, Studies and Surveys.* Annual. New York: FIND/SVP.

This directory lists more than 11,000 research reports, on a wide variety of industries, that were published by the best U.S. and European research firms. Also included are 1,400 company reports produced by investment firms. A midyear supplement updates the annual volume.

222. *Green Book: International Directory of Marketing Research Houses and Services.* Annual. New York: New York Chapter, American Marketing Assn.

The alphabetical arrangement of research organizations includes basic information and a description of the services offered. The five indexes provide access by company services, market/industry specialties, computer programs available, geographical arrangement of companies, and names of principal personnel.

223. Huffman, Robert J., and Watkins, Mary Michele. *Research Services Directory.* 3d ed. Detroit, MI: Gale Research Co., 1987. 641 p.

More than 3,400 fee- or contract-based organizations that provide research services including data collection and design, forecasting, surveys, and statistical studies are arranged alphabetically. Geographic, personal name, and subject indexes are provided. Kept up to date by *Research Services Directory: Supplement* which lists newly formed research services.

224. *MRA Research Service Directory.* Biannual. Chicago: Marketing Research Assn.

An alphbetical and geographical listing of research companies and field services in United States that indicates capabilities and facilities.

225. Watkins, Mary Michele; Dresser, Peter D.; and Huffman, Robert J., eds. *Research Centers Directory.* 11th ed. Detroit, MI: Gale Research Co., 1987. 2 vols. 1,770 p.

More than 9,200 university-related and other permanent nonprofit research organizations are listed alphabetically in four broad areas, including the address, governance, fields of research, and publications. Separate alphabetical, institutional, subject, special capabilities, and acronym indexes are provided. Kept up to date by *New Research Centers,* a supplement containing newly established organizations.

GUIDEBOOKS/HANDBOOKS

226. Alreck, Pamela L., and Settle, Robert B. *The Survey Research Handbook.* Homewood, IL: Richard D. Irwin, Inc., 1985. 429 p.

Coverage includes methods, techniques, activities, and skills needed to do effective survey research. This includes survey planning and design, choosing survey instruments, data collection and processing, analysis, and reporting.

227. Blankenship, Albert Breneman. *Professional Telephone Surveys.* New York: Prentice-Hall, 1977. 244 p.
For the individual unfamiliar with telephone surveys, this book provides and evaluates these surveys by explaining techniques, uses, and ways to contract for a survey.

228. Breen, George Edward, and Blankenship, Albert Breneman. *Do-It-Yourself Marketing Research.* 2d ed. New York: McGraw-Hill, 1982. 303 p.
A practical guide for the nonprofessional market researcher that explains how to conduct market studies necessary for making decisions in a small business, giving enough information so that the individual can decide when professional help is needed.

229. Dillman, Don A. *Mail and Telephone Surveys: The Total Design Method.* New York: Wiley, 1978. 325 p.
A step-by-step method of conducting successful mail and telephone surveys that provides new opportunities for survey research because it replaces the costly face-to-face interview. A bibliography provides additional sources of information.

230. Dutka, Solomon. *Notes on Statistical Sampling.* New York: Audits & Surveys, 1982. 268 p.
A review of sample survey designs covers cost efficiency and applications. Basics include sample survey design and topics such as simple random and stratified random sampling, sub-sampling techniques, and sampling of rare populations. Measuring response error, ratio and regression estimates, nonreponse implications, and hypothesis testing are included.

231. Dutka, Solomon; Frankel, Lester; and Roshwalb, Irving. *How to Conduct Surveys.* New York: Audits & Surveys, 1982. 197 p.
A step-by-step guide to planning and carrying out a survey project that covers many problems that arise in the collection, presentation, analysis, and interpretation of data. The establishment of survey objective, sample selection, questionnaire design, interviewing techniques, analysis, and reporting results are covered.

232. Ferber, Robert. *Handbook of Marketing Research.* New York: McGraw-Hill, 1974. Various paging.
This is a basic source for marketing research methods, techniques, and applications, intended for the researcher or marketing executive. The chapters on methodology present information in a nontechnical way, followed by a technical discussion for the advanced researcher.

233. Haley, Russell I. *Developing Effective Communications Strategy: A Benefit Segmentation Approach.* New York: Wiley, 1985. 510 p.
Locating an effective communication strategy, executing it, and determining the effect upon the market is the central issue of this book. Some of the areas covered include measuring attitudes and images, organizing and conducting segmentation research, interpreting results, and follow through activities for copy research, media, sales promotion, and pricing.

234. Kelly, John M. *How to Check Out the Competition: A Complete Plan for Investigating Your Market.* New York: Wiley, 1987. 275 p.
A complete guide for designing and implementing a competitor intelligence program covering areas such as research techniques to gather information, organization of information using work sheets, evaluating a competitors operations, administrations, and financial condition.

235. Pope, Jeffery L. *Practical Marketing Research.* New York: AMACOM, 1981. 269 p.

Focus is on application of marketing research techniques to problems, real-world issues, or how to get things done by providing information for those responsible for the research function. Some areas covered include packaging, advertising, sales testing, and product concept.

236. Rossi, Peter H.; Wright, James D.; and Anderson, Andy B. *Handbook of Survey Research.* New York: Academic Press, Inc., 1983. 755 p.

For both the student and those involved in research, this book covers major issues in designing a survey and an advanced level of analysis. As a detailed guide, both theory and practice are covered.

237. Ruddick, Morris E.; Sherwood, Philip K.; and Stevens, Robert E. *The Marketing Research Handbook: A Decision-Oriented Approach.* Englewood Cliffs, NJ: Prentice-Hall, 1983. 210 p.

Essential concepts and techniques are presented in concise form, and theoretical concepts are practically oriented. Examples of a research proposal, a questionnaire, and final report are included.

238. Schwerin, Horace S. and Newell, Henry H. *Persuasion in Marketing: The Dynamics of Marketing's Great Untapped Resource.* New York: Wiley, 1981. 259 p.

Persuasion is seen as total strategy which involves a systematic step-by-step program based on identifying changing consumer needs and how to meet them. This approach is used to understand the consumer market, life cycle of products, and the development of prototypes of campaigns.

239. Twedt, Dik Warren. *1983 Survey of Marketing Research: Organization, Functions, Budget, Compensation.* Chicago: American Marketing Assn., 1983. 66 p.

This is the seventh report in a series that began in 1947, and it updates the 1973 report. It provides a means of evaluating the organization of market research departments, research activities, budgets, and job compensation levels.

240. Vichas, Robert P. *Complete Handbook of Profitable Marketing Research Techniques.* Englewood Cliffs, NJ: Prentice-Hall, 1982. 432 p.

Forty basic marketing research techniques that are practical, productive, and economical for even the smallest companies include applications, forms, checklists, and questionnaires.

241. Worcester, Robert M., and Downham, John, eds. *Consumer Market Research Handbook.* New York: North-Holland, 1986. 840 p.

Part one provides a clear description of what is involved in designing, carrying out, and applying market research by explaining the techniques involved. Part two describes the way in which marketing research is applied to marketing and business problems.

PAPERS—COLLECTED

242. Jain, Arun K.; Pinson, Christian; and Ratchford, Brian T. *Marketing Research: Applications and Problems.* New York: Wiley, 1982. 555 p.

The two areas covered are issues in data collection and data analysis techniques. The papers cover the key marketing research tools and their applications. A variety of applications of multivariate techniques are included.

243. Peter, J. Paul, and Ray, Michael L. comps. *Measurement Readings for Marketing Research.* Chicago: American Marketing Assn., 1984. 374 p.

Designed for marketing researchers, this book provides a resource to better measure development and investigation procedures. Papers cover the contributions from psychology, an overview of the reliability and validity of marketing research, and selected representative measurement studies in marketing.

PERIODICALS/ANNUALS

244. *American Demographics.* 10/yr. Ithaca, NY: American Demographics, Inc.

Articles on all aspects of demography include developments, analysis, population shifts, trends, and data sources.

245. *The Information Catalog.* Bimonthly. New York: FIND/SVP.

This is an annotated list of industry studies, company reports, and business and marketing books that provide information on areas such as competitive intelligence, market trends, product positioning, emerging growth markets, consumer attitudes, and technological developments.

246. *International Journal of Research in Marketing.* Quarterly. Amsterdam, The Netherlands: North-Holland.

The aim of this official journal of the European Marketing Academy is to integrate theoretical and empirical research for insights into the factors determining marketing mechanisms and practices. Emphasis is on European research involving different disciplinary approaches covering areas such as profit and nonprofit marketing, consumer behavior, product, decisions, and strategic market planning.

247. *Journal of Data Collection: A Publication of Applied Marketing Research.* Semiannual. Chicago: Marketing Research Assn.

An important source for applied marketing research information that includes articles and interviews focusing on the latest technology and information.

248. *Journal of the Market Research Society.* Quarterly. London: Market Research Society.

Papers and short notices focus on practical applications, evaluation of specific problem areas, and broad marketing fields and social research.

249. *Market Research Abstracts.* Semiannual. London: The Market Research Society.

Abstracts of articles from approximately forty British and American periodicals cover all fields of marketing with relevant articles from economics, statistics, sociology, and psychology arranged by broad subject groups. Specific subject indexes are provided.

250. *Marketing/Advertising/Research.* Bimonthly. New York: Business/Professional Advertising Assn.

This newsletter carries how-to articles on conducting marketing research and advertising studies, including techniques and evaluations.

251. *The Nielsen Researcher.* Irregular. Northbrook, IL: Nielsen Market Research.

Consumer research, product cycles, use of scanning data, industry brands, and promotion evaluation are a few of the areas covered in recent issues. Graphs and charts accompany most articles, some of which are adaptation of association/organization presentations.

252. *Research Alert: A Bi-Weekly Report of Consumer Marketing Studies.* Bi-weekly. New York: MIN Publishing, Inc.

Abstracts of consumer marketing studies cover a wide range of topics and include the name of the group that commissioned the survey and the issue and page number in which the article appeared.

253. Sheth, Jagdish N., ed. *Research in Marketing: A Research Annual.* Annual. Greenwich, CT: JAI Press, Inc.

Original essays on new and significant research on various aspects of marketing are in each volume of this series.

PROCEEDINGS

254. Chasin, Joseph, ed. *Straight Talk about Attitude Research.* Chicago: American Marketing Assn., 1982. 225 p.

Papers presented at the annual Attitude Research Conference cover various topics of consumer behavior and attitudes, advertising research, structuring of markets, and cognitive response.

255. Keon, John W., ed. *Market Measurement and Analysis: Proceedings of the Third ORSA/TIMS Special Interest Conference on Market Measurements and Analysis.* Providence, RI: TIMS College on Marketing, The Insitute of Management Sciences and the Operations Research Society, 1981. 283 p.

Papers presented at the conference cover various aspects of market measures and market analysis.

256. Montgomery, David B., and Wittink, Dick R. *Market Measurement and Analysis: Proceedings of the First ORSA/TIMS Special Interest Conference, March 26-28, 1979.* Cambridge, MA: Marketing Science Institute, 1980. 573 p.

The research papers in this collection cover the theoretical developments and managerial applications for a variety of topics related to measurement and analysis of markets. Some topics are the measurement of response, sales forecasting, market segmentation, managerial decision making, models of consumer values, attitudes, and purchase behavior.

257. Olshavsky, Richard W., ed. *Attitude Research Enters the 80's.* Chicago: American Marketing Assn., 1980. 196 p.

Papers presented at the Attitude Research Conference cover new theories and methods of data collection, relationship between attitude and behavior, and the application of attitude research to marketing and public policy.

258. *Seminar on Sampling Problems and Data Collection—Special Target Groups: Copenhagen, Denmark, 20-22nd May, 1981.* Amsterdam, The Netherlands: European Society for Opinion and Marketing Research, 1981. 179 p.

A collection of papers covering various topics on consumer research such as small sector research, sampling businessmen, and rare target groups. The section on industrial research covers industrial sampling, the role of prior data in sampling minority populations, and optimizing newspaper sales.

STATISTICAL INFORMATION

Guidebooks/Handbooks

259. Frank, Nathalie D., and Ganly, John V. *Data Sources for Business and Market Analysis.* 3d ed. Metuchen, NJ: Scarecrow Press, Inc., 1983. 470 p.

This annotated bibliography of original sources of quantitative data, secondary data, and sources of business information covers economic conditions, business trends, consumer, and industrial markets. The emphasis is on serial publications with 1982 the cutoff date.

260. O'Hara, Frederick M., and Sicignano, Robert. *Handbook of United States Economic and Financial Indicators.* Westport, CT: Greenwood Press, 1985. 224 p.

U.S. government statistical series covering inflation measures, profits, financial indicators, interest rates, employment, unemployment, and earnings are described in detail. These explanations cover how they are compiled, strengths and weaknesses, and where to call for additional information.

Indexes

261. *American Statistics Index: A Comprehensive Guide and Index to Statistical Publications of the U.S. Government.* Monthly with annual cumulations. Bethesda, MD: Congressional Information Service, Inc.

This is the best source for most of the statistical publications of government agencies, congressional committees, and statistics producing programs. A detailed subject index and category, geographic area, title of report, and report number indexes are provided. The numbers in the indexes refer to the abstract which has a complete description of the publication and details about the statistical data. Microfiche copy of many of the items is a part of the service.

262. *Statistical Reference Index: A Selective Guide to American Statistical Publications from Private Organizations and State Government Sources.* Monthly with annual cumulations. Washington, DC: Congressional Information Service.

Publications of associations, business and independent research organizations, state governments, and universities are indexed by subjects, names, categories, issuing sources, and titles. The index section provides the item number for location of the abstract of the information. Microfiche copy of many of the items is a part of this publication. An excellent source for marketing information.

263. U.S. Department of Commerce. *Statistical Abstract of the United States.* 106th ed. Annual. Washington, DC: U.S. Government Printing Office, 1986.

A handy compilation of statistics covering most areas of the U.S. economy, including demographics, labor, business enterprises, transportation, manufacturers, and communications. Sources for the tables are given if more up-to-date information is needed. Some tables have historical series.

Economic Conditions

264. *Business Conditions Digest.* Monthly. Washington, DC: U.S. Bureau of Economic Analysis, U.S. Government Printing Office.

Graphic and tabular presentations of data about current economic conditions include the leading economic time series of use to business analysts and forecasters.

265. *Economic Indicators.* Monthly. Washington, DC: U.S. Government Printing Office.

A monthly publication of statistical charts and tables for basic economic indicators that includes annual data for six to eight years, and monthly data for the last year in areas such as gross national product, personal consumption expenditures, production and business activity, prices, money, and credit.

266. *Economic Outlook USA.* Quarterly. Ann Arbor, MI: Survey Research Center, University of Michigan.

Designed for the decision maker, the data presents the economic and social environment of the United States. This publication measures attitudes and expectations of consumers and business people and includes actual short-term and projected economic development.

267. *Statistical Bulletin.* Monthly. New York: Conference Board.

Marketing indicators such as discretionary spending and consumer confidence are given along with other tables and charts for basic economic indicators. Tabular forecasts from eight econometric firms and university forecasting organizations are included.

Geographical Analysis

268. *County Business Patterns.* Annual. Washington, DC: U.S. Bureau of the Census, U.S. Government Printing Office.

Separate issues for each state and a U.S. summary list for each four-digit SIC number, county totals of number of employees, taxable payrolls, and number of establishments by employment size. Useful for analyzing market potential, but the figures are not up to date.

269. Editor & Publisher Co. *Market Guide.* Annual. New York.

Demographic and business data for more than 1,600 U.S. and Canadian daily newspaper cities are arranged alphabetically by city within the state or province. Metropolitan Statistical Area rankings are included.

270. *Forecasting Service.* Annual. New York: Sales & Marketing Management Magazine, 1983.

Market facts and projections for the next decade include state and regional summaries, metropolitan market rankings, demographic and income data, and retail sales for metropolitan markets and counties. TV markets and sales are also given.

271. *MEI Marketing Economics Guide.* Annual. New York: Marketing Economics Institute, Ltd.

The institute has an extensive database of demographic, economic, and retail sales data that is the basis for the statistical information in this guide. Population, retail trade, merchandise lines, and consumer expenditures cover every country, SMSA, and more than 2,300 cities.

272. *MPA: Market Profile Analysis.* Annual. New York: Financial Service Group of Donnelley Marketing Services.

A computer printout that is useful for evaluating the existing locations as well as proposed sites of stores, branches, or outlets. Also useful for market research and long-range planning. Tabular information covers retail market trends, financial development, and construction activity presented by SMSA, broken down by ZIP code.

273. *Rand McNally Commercial Atlas and Marketing Guide.* Annual. Chicago: Rand McNally & Co., 1986. 589 p.

This atlas has economic and geographical information that includes stastical data and interpretations for business usage. ZIP code marketing data tables and maps of trading areas, of retail sales, of manufacturing and Metropolitan Statistical Areas with accompanying statistical tables are included. Data tables for every county in the U.S. cover population, household and retail sales, and wholesale trade statistics. Useful for regional market studies.

274. *Rand McNally Sales & Marketing Atlas: Vital Information for Market Analysis, Sales Planning, Territory Management, Distribution and Traffic Control and Much More.* Annual. Chicago: Rand McNally & Co.

More than 18,000 places with a population of 1,000 or more are listed alphabetically by state. State indexes that precede each map include counties, military installations, county seats, multicounty places, unincorporated places, and independent cities.

275. *Rand McNally ZIP Code Atlas: The Reliable Atlas for Zip Code Areas as Marketing Units.* Chicago: Rand McNally & Co., 1983. 152 p.

ZIP code areas are alternative marketing units to county divisions and this atlas provides a quick way to locate this information. The three-digit ZIP code areas are printed in red and overlay the county divisions on the outlined state maps. For each ZIP code in the state, marketing data such as number of households, retail, and wholesale trade sales are given. Sixteen large cities have five-digit ZIP code maps.

276. *Sourcebook of Demographics and Buying Power for Every ZIP Code in the USA.* Annual. Arlington, VA: CACI.

Data for this publication are based on CACAI's geodemographic database which is updated annually to include proprietary current year estimates and five-year projections. The residential section, divided by state, includes demographic, population, and socioeconomic profiles for each ZIP code in numerical order. The business section lists ZIP codes in numerical sequence, including information on the number of firms, estimated employment, and ranking by top five SIC numbers.

Industry Analysis

277. *Predicasts Basebook.* Annual. Cleveland, OH: Predicasts, Inc.

Coverage of about fourteen years with approximately 28,000 series arranged by modified SIC number covering production, consumption, sales, wholesale price, plant, and equipment. The average yearly growth rates is also given.

278. *Predicasts Forecasts.* Quarterly. Annual cumulations. Cleveland, OH: Predicasts, Inc.

Short- and long-range forecasts that cover economic indicators, industries' products, and services are from a wide variety of printed sources. These are arranged by modified SIC numbers with the source of the forecast included.

279. *Standard & Poor's Industry Surveys.* Quarterly. New York: Standard & Poor's Corp.

General information on various industries with composite industry data and statistics, market activity, company analyses, and specific product segmentation. The *Trends and Projections* section analyzes the U.S. economy and includes forecasts for various economic indicators.

280. *Survey of Current Business.* Monthly. Washington, DC: U.S. Bureau of Economic Analysis, U.S. Government Printing Office.
An important source for business statistics. The monthly covers general business indicators and statistics on various products. A biennial supplement, *Business Statistics*, is a historical record of statistics in the monthly issues.

281. U.S. Bureau of the Census. *Census of Manufacturers.* Every 5 years. Washington, DC: U.S. Government Printing Office.
Statistical data on 452 SIC classifications for manufacturing industries covering items such as number of establishments, employment, payrolls, quantity and value of products shipped, and materials used. The information is arranged in three volumes by subject, industry, and geographic area. The *Annual Survey of Manufacturers* is a sample survey. *Current Industrial Reports* covers about 5,000 manufactured products with data on production, shipments, and inventories.

282. *U.S. Industrial Outlook.* Annual. Washington, DC: U.S. Bureau of Industrial Economics, Department of Commerce, U.S. Government Printing Office.
This publication provides information on recent trends and outlook for five years in advance for 350 manufacturing and service industries. Statistical information covers the current situation, price, markets, and long-term prospects. No specific company information is included.

ASSOCIATIONS

American Associaton for Public Opinion Research. P.O. Box 17, Princeton, NJ 08542.

Center for Marketing Strategy Research. 3629 Locust Walk, Philadelphia, PA 19104.

Consumer Research Center. The Conference Board, Inc., 845 Third Avenue, New York, NY 10022.

Market Research Assn. 221 N. LaSalle St., Chicago, IL 60601.

Advertising

ABSTRACTS

283. *Communication Abstracts.* Quarterly. Beverly Hills, CA: Sage Publications.
Abstracts of communication-related journal articles, reports, books, and book chapters cover fields of advertising, broadcasting, communications, newspapers, and other related areas.

BIBLIOGRAPHIES

284. Lipstein, Benjamin, and McGuire, William J. *Evaluating Advertising: A Bibliography of the Communication Process.* New York: Advertising Research Foundation, 1978. 362 p.
More than 7,000 citations to research relevant to the creation and evaluation of persuasive communication include books and journals. An alphabetical list of access words and a topic index are included. The author index has the annotated citations.

DATABASES

285. Adtrack. 1980–84. St. Paul, MN: The Kingman Consulting Group, Inc. (Vendor: DIAL)
Advertisements covering quarter-page size of more than 100 U.S. consumer magazines are indexed by product name, company name, characteristics, and contents of the ad. The database is designed for advertising agencies, product and brand managers, and retailers.

286. Information Bank Advertising & Marketing Intelligence Service. 1979–. New York: The New York Times Co. (Vendor: Mead)
Daily updates from sixty major trade and professional publications covering market research, consumer behavior, product safety, new product, sales promotions, and other related information. Also includes statistical data for sales, market shares, sales promotions, and demographics.

287. PTS Marketing and Advertising Reference Service (PTS MARS). 1984–. Cleveland, OH: Predicasts, Inc.
Abstracts of articles from advertising journals and newspapers that cover marketing and advertising of consumer goods, advertising agency news, promotional campaigns, media use, trends and statistics, target markets, consumer attitudes, and related topics are searchable.

DICTIONARIES

288. *Ayer Glossary of Advertising and Related Terms.* 2d ed. Philadelphia, PA: Ayer Press, 1977. 219 p.

The general section of the glossary has definitions on all the terms, which are also listed in separate sections of TV and radio terms; printing, photography, and graphic art terms; computer and data processing terms.

289. Graham, Irvin. *Encyclopedia of Advertising.* 2d ed. New York: Fairchild Publications, 1969. 494 p.

More than 1,100 entries covering advertising, marketing, publishing, law, research, public relations, publicity, and the graphic arts are included. Useful for older terms, but it does not reflect newer words or concepts.

290. Imber, Jane, and Toffler, Betsy-Ann. *Dictionary of Advertising and Direct Mail Terms.* New York: Barron's Educational Series, 1987. 500 p.

Definitions of almost 3,000 terms used in television, radio, print, and direct mail advertising industries are included in this dictionary.

291. Paetzel, Hans W. *Complete Multilingual Dictionary of Advertising, Marketing and Communications.* Lincolnwood, IL: Passport Books, 1984. 606 p.

More than 8,000 technical and general communication terms in German, English, and French are listed in three columns to the page. Each language section has the equivalent term in the other two languages.

292. Urdang, Laurence, ed. *Dictionary of Advertising.* Lincolnwood, IL: NTC Business Books, 1986. 209 p.

The more than 4,000 terms listed are special meaning words or the jargon in day-to-day use in advertising agencies and corporations. In addition, services, organizations, and abbreviations and acronyms are included.

DIRECTORIES

293. *Adweek's Marketer's Guide to Media.* Quarterly. New York: A/S/M Communications.

A handy, pocket-sized reference guide that gives approximate costs for commercial and cable television, magazine, radio, and newspaper advertising. Audience estimates, profiles, and trends are also included.

294. *Black Media Directory.* Irregular. Livingston, NJ: Burrelle's Media Directories.

Print media covers national newspapers, periodicals, syndicated columns, college publications, state and local newspapers, and periodicals. Broadcasting media lists networks, television, and radio stations.

295. *Broadcasting/Cablecasting Yearbook.* Annual. Washington, DC: Broadcasting Publications.

A directory to radio, TV stations, cable systems, satellites, programming, advertising, and marketing agencies handling major TV accounts. The "Television Marketplace" section defines each television marketplace in relation to the viewing audience in surrounding counties.

296. *The Buyers Guide to Outdoor Advertising.* Biannual. New York: Institute of Outdoor Advertising.

Arranged by state, the current rates and market statistics for standardized "Poster Medium" and "Rotary Painted" displays are provided in this loose-leaf directory.

297. *Circulation: The Comprehensive Print Analysis Showing Circulation and Penetration.* Annual. Malibu, CA: American Newspaper Markets, Inc.

Coverage includes circulation data on every U.S. county, metro area, and television viewing area for daily and Sunday newspaper, regional sales groups, five national supplements, and twenty-three leading magazines. The listing includes population, households, retail sales, and average household income. The changes in the U.S. Bureau of the Census designation of Consolidated Metropolitan Statistical Areas (CMSA) and Metropolitan Statistical Areas (MSA) are explained in the preface.

298. *Co-Op Source Directory: A Guide to Cooperative Advertising Programs.* Semiannual. Wilmette, IL: Standard Rate & Data Service.

Manufacturer's co-op advertising programs vary considerably. This listing of more than 3,800 programs in a classified arrangement provides a summary of retailer, reseller, and wholesaler advertising plans. Classification, manufacturers, and trademark indexes are provided.

299. *Handbook of Advertising and Marketing Services.* Annual. New York: Executive Communications.

A directory of services, consultants, and experts in all areas of marketing including advertising, broadcasting, and communications. Each entry concisely summarizes the service experience, expertise, type of clients, performance records, and contact persons of the company. A listing by major and subcategories is provided.

300. *Madison Avenue Handbook.* Annual. New York: Peter Glenn Publications.

A directory of advertising services and marketing areas throughout the U.S. that lists companies supplying media, film, video photography, illustration/design, photography, and allied services.

301. Mossman, Jennifer, and Wood, Donna, eds. *Business Firms Master Index: A Guide to Sources of Information on Approximately 110,000 Companies in the United States and Including Canadian and Other Selected Foreign Firms.* Detroit, MI: Gale Research Co., 1985. 1,124 p.

A guide to sources of information on companies that are in the field of communication which includes advertising agencies, cable networks, computer companies, publishers, radio and TV stations, and related companies. The companies are listed alphabetically with the abbreviated citation to the source indexed. Updated by the *Business Firms Master Index: Supplement* which adds about 25,000 new citations to published sources of information.

302. *Standard Directory of Advertisers.* Annual. Wilmette, IL: National Register Publishing Co.

A directory of more than 17,000 companies that advertise nationally, arranged by industry. Each entry includes officers, product names, advertising agency, media used, and the advertising budget for some of the companies. Tradename and alphabetical indexes are provided. The *Geographic Index* is a separate volume. *Ad-Change,* a biweekly publication, updates the basic volume, and the bimonthly *Supplement* cumulates this information in *Ad-Change.*

303. *Standard Directory of Advertising Agencies: The Advertising Red Book.* 3/yr. Wilmette, IL: National Register Publishing Co.

Approximately 4,800 advertising agencies are included in this directory. Each listing includes the usual directory information, lists association memberships, the area of specialization, annual billings with breakdown by type of media, and the accounts or companies serviced by the agency.

304. *Women's Media Directory.* Irregular. Livingston, NJ: Burrelle's Media Directories.

More than 500 listings of print and broadcast media cover periodicals, sydicated columns, and newspapers. The media covers television and radio stations that have regularly scheduled shows oriented toward women.

GUIDEBOOKS/HANDBOOKS

305. Barban, Arnold M. *Advertising Media Sourcebook.* 2d ed. Columbus, OH: Grid, Inc., 1981. 169 p.

A guide to information on advertising media that leads the planner from objectives to strategy to making media decisions. The explanations of the technical aspects of media are helpful.

306. Bly, Robert W. *Create the Perfect Sales Piece: How to Produce Brochures, Catalogs, Fliers and Pamphlets.* New York: Wiley, 1985. 242 p.

This do-it-yourself guide to producing promotional literature tells how to create printed material that fits a company's image and budget. Sample illustrations of various types of publications, visual aids, typefaces, art work, worksheets, and checklists are included.

307. Crimmins, Edward C. *Cooperative Advertising: A Comprehensive Guide for Managers Who Make Decisions about This Dynamic Marketing Tool.* New York: Gene Wolfe & Co., Inc., 1984. 197 p.

The theoretical and practical aspects of cooperative advertising in this book are aimed at manufacturers, other suppliers of cooperative advertising programs, intermediate sellers of manufacturers products, and members of the media. The legal aspects, objectives of this program, variations in products, customers, market coverage, percentage of participation, budgeting, writing, and implementing the programs are discussed.

308. Fletcher, Alan D., and Bowers, Thomas A. *Fundamentals of Advertising Research.* 2d ed. Columbus, OH: Grid, 1983. 343 p.

A how-to book covering marketing research techniques, interpretations, and applications, including the methodology of advertising research, gathering data, selecting samples, conducting research, and writing the report.

309. Johnson, Philip M. *How to Maximize Your Advertising Investment.* Boston: CBI, 1980. 226 p.

To maximize return on advertising investment, it is important to have realistic objectives and strategies for advertsing to the target audience. Monitoring the market plan, measurement and merchandising, personal advertising, and using an ad agency are some topics covered.

310. Kaatz, Ronald B. *Cable Advertiser's Handbook.* 2d ed. Lincolnwood, IL: Crain Books, 1986.

This handbook covers evaluating audiences, buying time, creating effective advertising, merchandising at the local and national level, and measuring advertising effectiveness in the expanding cable industry.

311. Murphy, Jonne. *Handbook of Radio Advertising.* Radnor, PA: Chilton Books, 1980. 240 p.
This guide covers selling, buying, and planning radio advertising for national advertisers and local retailers.

312. Rust, Ronald T. *Advertising Media Models: A Practical Guide.* Lexington, MA: Lexington Books, 1986. 159 p.
A practical how-to guide that analyzes the media-planning process and suggests where to find information for making cost-effective media decisions.

313. Schwerin, Horace S., and Newell, Henry H. *Persuasion in Marketing: The Dynamics of Marketing's Great Untapped Resource.* New York: Wiley, 1981. 259 p.
This book deals with more than testing of advertising because it covers the entire marketing process. Understanding the consumers needs, development of marketing strategy, pretesting the strategy, making the media choice, and the post-evaluation of the strategy is based on persuasion, which is a modification of present company selling practices.

314. Stansfield, Richard H. *The Dartnell Advertising Manager's Handbook.* 3d ed. Chicago: Dartnell Corp. 1982. 1,088 p.
The practical information in this publication covers 2,600 separate subjects and contains over 500 illustrations, case histories of ad campaigns, creative copy, tips on choosing the right media, planning a budget, and more.

315. Surmanek, Jim. *Media Planning: A Practical Guide.* Lincolnwood, IL: Crain Books, 1985. 165 p.
Selecting the right media mix is important, and that includes defining demographic targets and evaluating the dynamics of various media forms to select advertising that meets the marketing objectives. Also covered are analyzing research and budgeting for advertising.

316. Weilbacher, William M. *Choosing an Advertising Agency.* Chicago: Crain Books, 1983. 170 p.
Whether changing agencies or hiring one for the first time, this guide explains how to establish a search group, write an account profile, determine selection criteria, develop a fact sheet, and evaluate agency presentations.

PERIODICALS/ANNUALS

317. *Advertising Age.* Semiweekly. Chicago: Crain Communications, Inc.
The basic trade journal for the advertising and marketing industry covers topics such as advertising expenditures, finances of advertising agencies, and consumer recall of advertising. Data are from company reports, trade associations, and private research firms. Special issues cover advertising agency profiles, leading media companies, leading national advertisers, leading market research firms. Annual tables and market shares for some products such as coffee, cold cereal, liquor, and wine are also included.

318. *Adweek: National Marketing Edition.* Weekly. New York: A/S/M Communications, Inc.
News and information at the national level for marketing executives and client companies, with extensive use of illustration, creativity, and photography to illustrate the features.

319. *Adweek/Midwest.* Weekly. Chicago: A/S/M Communications, Inc. *Adweek/ New England.* Weekly. Boston: A/S/M Communications, Inc. *Adweek/Southeast.* Weekly. Atlanta, GA: A/S/M Communications, Inc. *Adweek/Southwest.* Weekly. Dallas, TX: A/S/M Communications, Inc. *Adweek/West.* Weekly. Los Angeles: A/S/M Communications, Inc.

    These regional editions cover the advertising scene in each particular area. Each has an annual directory of advertisng agencies that includes information on billing, income, names of accounts gained or lost, media placement, and ranked lists of agencies.

320. *Business Publications Rates and Data.* Monthly. Wilmette, IL: Standard Rate and Data Service, Inc.

    Part one contains advertising rates for industrial, merchandising, professional, and house organs. Part two is a classified listing of publications. Part three is an index to direct-response advertising media and international business publications.

321. *Community Publications Rates and Data.* Monthly. Wilmette, IL: Standard Rate and Data Service, Inc.

    Advertising rates are given for the smaller community publications, daily, weekly, and monthly, and shopping guides.

322. *Consumer Magazines and Agri-Media Rates and Data.* Monthly. Wilmette, IL: Standard Rate and Data Service, Inc.

    Includes comprehensive market data for market analysis and comparison by geographic region, Metropolitan Statisical Area, Areas of Dominant Influence (ADI), and Designated Market Area (DMA). The magazines are listed in a classified arrangement.

323. *Co-Op News.* Biweekly. Wilmette, IL: Standard Rate & Data Service.

    A newspaper that covers cooperative advertising topics of interest to advertising agencies, the media, manufacturers, and retailers.

324. *Current Issues & Research in Advertising.* Annual. Ann Arbor, MI: Division of Research, Graduate School of Business Administration, University of Michigan.

    The purpose of this annual is to advance the state of the art in advertising theory, covering current developments and practices. Complete reports of original, theoretical research, and scholarly papers cover a wide range of topics of interest to academics

325. *Electronic Media.* Weekly. Chicago: Crain Communications, Inc.

    A tabloid newspaper that covers news and information on all types of electronic media, including cable television, radio programming, videotext, home video, and other emerging forms.

326. *Gallagher Report.* Weekly. New York: Gallagher Communications, Inc.

    For the advertising, marketing, media, and sales executive, this newsletter covers experts' views on business, trends, interpertation of events, and legislative developments.

327. *International Journal of Advertising: The Quarterly Review of Marketing Communications.* Quarterly. London: The Advertising Association.

    Articles can be research oriented, practice based, state of the art or polemical covering a wide range of topics such as consumer advertising, market research, public relations, industrial marketing, consumerism, role of the media, product management, and sales promotion.

328. *Journal of Advertising.* Quarterly. Laramie, WY: College of Commerce and Industry, University of Wyoming.

This scholarly journal of the American Academy of Advertising focuses on theoretical developments in the psychological and philosophical aspects of communication and the relationship of these to advertising.

329. *Journal of Advertising Research.* Bimonthly. New York: Advertising Research Foundation.

Intended for users and practitioners of advertising research, the focus of the articles is on advertising research and methodology. Reports of findings rather than theoretical discussions and studies that are not based on student samples are included.

330. *Madison Avenue.* Monthly. New York: Madison Avenue Magazine Publishing Corp.

Marketing thought and advertising strategy are covered in articles on advertising agencies, market segment advertising campaigns, successful and failed ad campaigns, and analysis of print and broadcast media. Concentration is on New York-based advertising.

331. *Marketing & Media Decisions.* Monthly. New York: Decisions Publications, Inc.

A practically oriented magazine that has feature articles covering print and electronic media, special reports on marketing a variety of products, advertising expenditures by products, and media cost forecasts. A special issue is devoted to the top market success of the year.

332. *Newspaper Rates and Data.* Monthly. Wilmette, IL: Standard Rate and Data Service, Inc.

Rates for advertising in daily, weekly, college, university, and black newspapers are given. Part two provides data on newspaper circulation and penetration in metro, TV market, and county areas, including market data and demographics.

333. *Spot Radio Rates and Data.* Monthly. Wilmette IL: Standard Rate and Data Service, Inc.

Advertising rates for larger radio markets, station listings, national, and regional networks are given. Market data on state, county, city, and metro areas and media/market maps are included in this publication.

334. *Spot Radio Small Markets Edition.* Monthly. Wilmette, IL: Standard Rate and Data Service, Inc.

Advertising rates for the radio stations in cities under 25,000 population are given in this edition.

335. *Spot Television Rates and Data.* Monthly. Wilmette, IL: Standard Rate and Data Service, Inc.

Rates for local station television advertising and statistical data on markets and consumers are included.

PROCEEDINGS

336. Houston, Michael J., and Lutz, Richard J., eds. *Marketing Communications: Theory and Research.* Chicago: American Marketing Assn., 1985. 220 p.

The papers presented at this conference convey the diversity of theories, topics, issues, and research procedures of those working with all types of marketing communication. Areas include advertising, interorganizational and intraorganizational communication, ethical issues, direct mail response techniques, and others.

337. Percy, Larry, and Woodside, Arch G., eds. *Advertising and Consumer Psychology.* Vol 1. Lexington, MA: Lexington Books, 1983.
The eighteen scholarly papers presented at a workshop sponsored in part by the Division of Consumer Psychology of the American Psychological Assocation are divided into the broad areas of how advertising, works, brain waves, cognitive and psychological response to advertising, and manipulating advertising variables.

STATISTICAL INFORMATION

338. *Ad$ Summary.* Quarterly with annual cumulations. New York: Leading National Advertisers.
The top 1,000 companies are ranked by total dollars spent on seven media, and by dollars spent on the separate media, which include magazines, newspaper supplement, network television, spot television, network radio, outdoor advertising, and cable TV networks. Also has alphabetical lists by brand names, with parent company name, and the dollars spent on that brand for advertising.

339. *Advertising Volume in the U.S.* Semiannual. New York: Television Bureau of Advertising.
This report covers national and local advertising in eight major media with data from the forties through the eighties for selected media.

340. *Arbitron Ratings: Radio.* Annual. New York: Arbitron Ratings Co.
Audience estimates in metropolitan areas of various cities provide statistical data, by sex and age, which is useful for evluating audience size and composition.

341. *Arbitron Ratings: Television. Geographic Market Planning Guide.* Annual. New York: Arbitron Rating Co.
Advertising dollars spent in the Area of Dominant Influence (ADI) has an effect on outside markets, and this report furnishes television stations, advertisers, and agency clients with an aid to buying and selling decisions.

342. *Key Facts about Newspapers and Advertising.* Annual. New York: Newspaper Advertising Bureau.
Socioeconomic data on newspaper audiences, advertising expenditures/sales ratio for some retail and service industries, and national and local advertising expenditures are some of the areas covered.

343. *MRI: Mediamark Research, Inc.* Annual. New York: Mediamark Research, Inc.
A multivolume set that has detailed demographic information and market segmentation of media audiences in relation to products. This information is used by advertising agencies, magazines, and other media in determining market targets and in guiding market strategy.

344. *Simmons Study of Media and Markets.* Annual. New York: Simmons Market Research Bureau.
Data on the size, composition of reading, viewing and listening audiences, relation of these to each other and to the target markets are included. Detailed descriptions and characteristics of users of individual brands, products, and services are included, along with demographic information.

345. *Television ADI Market Guide.* Annual. New York: Arbitron Ratings Co.
Statistical data on media and audience profiles covers demographic characteristics, by household and counties, sales and marketing statistics and is arranged by central city. Description of data and sources is also included.

ASSOCIATIONS

Advertising Research Foundation. 3 E. 54th St., New York, NY 10022.

American Academy of Advertising, Department of Advertising. University of Illinois, 810 S. Wright, Urbana, IL 61801.

American Advertising Federation. 1225 Connecticut Ave., N.W., Washington, DC 20036.

American Association of Advertising Agencies. 666 Third Ave., 13th Floor, New York, NY 10017.

Association of National Advertisers, Inc. 155 E. 44th St., New York, NY 10017.

Business/Professional Advertising Association. 205 E. 42nd St., New York, NY 10017.

Newspaper Advertising Bureau. 1180 Avenue of the Americas, New York, NY 10036.

Television Bureau of Advertising. 477 Madison Ave., New York, NY 10022.

Women in Advertising and Marketing. 4200 Wisconsin Ave., N.W., Suite 106-238, Washington, DC 20016.

Business/Industrial and Government Marketing

BIBLIOGRAPHIES

346. Pingry, Jack R., and Bird, Monroe Murphy. *Industrial Marketing: A Selected and Annotated Bibliography.* Chicago: American Marketing Assn., 1977. 71 p.

Various aspects of industrial marketing including purchasing management and buyer behavior, product policy, channels of distribution, industrial promotion and advertising, pricing, and marketing research are covered in this bibliography.

DIRECTORIES

347. *Directory of Manufacturers Agents National Association.* Annual. Laguna Hills, CA: Manufacturers Agents National Assn.

Manufacturers who are associate members of this association are listed alphabetically in the first section. Separate sections have product, manufacturers and agents, and state listings.

348. Hong, Alfred, ed. *MEI: Marketing Economics Key Plants: Guide to Industrial Purchasing Power.* Biannual. New York: Marketing Economics Institute.

A two-part directory that lists more than 40,000 plants with 100 or more employees by state, by county, and by SIC number in each county. The second part lists companies by SIC and within each industry by state and county. Only address, phone, SIC number, and employment range is given. The plant listings make this a potentially useful marketing tool.

GUIDEBOOKS/HANDBOOKS

349. *Advertising Research.* New York: Business/Professional Advertising Association, 1983. 70 p.

This handbook provides practical how-to advice by answering the questions most frequently asked in connection with business-to-business advertising. Areas covered include media readership surveys, measuring communications, inquiries as a research tool, pretesting advertising, sample size, and mail surveys.

350. Berry, Dick. *Industrial Marketing for Results.* Reading, MA: Addison-Wesley, 1981. 210 p.

Intended for executives in industrial companies, this practical book shows how to combine marketing variables to serve customers and gain marketing advantage. Marketing concepts and principles are illustrated with many examples. Topics include information sources, marketing management and strategy, strengthening product distribution, pricing for profit, marketing planning, and forecasting.

351. Bonoma, Thomas V., and Shapiro, Benson P. *Industrial Market Segmentation: A Nested Approach.* Cambridge, MA: Marketing Science Institute, 1983. 120 p.

The interlocking segmentation nest approach covers demographics, operating variables, purchasing approaches, situational factors, personal characteristics, application of marketing segmentation schemes, and controlling implementation.

352. Cox, William E. *Industrial Marketing Research.* New York: Wiley, 1979. 468 p.

This book concentrates on industrial goods and markets, minimizing duplication of research methods, and theories in books oriented toward consumer goods and markets. Data methods, responsibilities of industrial marketing research, surveys, and quantitative and behavioral models are covered.

353. Hague, Paul N. *The Industrial Market Research Handbook.* London: Kogan Page, 1985. 356 p.

For those unfamiliar with the role of marketing or market research, this book explains project organization and methods of market research. The checklists increase the value of this book.

354. Hofsoos, Emil. *What Management Should Know about Industrial Advertising.* Houston, TX: Gulf Publishing Co., 1970. 122 p.

The principles, practice, and guidelines of an industrial advertising program are covered. Goals, ideas, media, corporate image, and measuring advertising results are some areas discussed.

355. Inzinga, Donna A. Project Manager. *Business/Industrial Direct Marketing.* New York: Direct Mail/Marketing, 1982. 312 p.

The techniques for developing a business/industrial direct marketing approach are covered. Included are developing direct marketing strategy, the planning process, overview of target markets, and the media to use, business lists, use of computers, integration of the sales force, testing, and analysis.

356. Jackson, Barbara Bund. *Winning and Keeping Industrial Customers: The Dynamics of Customer Relationships.* Lexington, MA: Lexington Books, 1985. 195 p.

This book explores the time dimension of industrial marketing relationships covering switching costs and exposure, time dimensions of marketing tools, strengthening customer's commitments, cascaded demand, and making concepts work.

357. Kelleher, Robert F. *Industrial Marketing and Sales Management in the Computer Age.* Boston: CBI Publishing Co., 1982. 172 p.

A formal, decision-oriented, computer-based information system provides the manager with an important means of increasing market productivity. How-to explanations cover the development of a system covering analysis of market productivity, managing costs, providing for customer file support, and intelligence gathering. Sample questionnaires are included.

358. Krigman, Alan. *Researching Industrial Markets: How to Identify, Reach and Sell to Your Customers.* Research Triangle Park, NC: Instrument Society of America, 1983. 80 p.

The practical research processes that are useful for generating market information are covered including lists of sources in the appendices. The use of the information in sales, product planning and development, marketing strategy decisions, and product promotions are based on the realities of the marketing process.

359. Lee, Donald D. *Industrial Marketing Research: Techniques and Practices.* 2d ed. New York: Van Nostrand Reinhold, 1984. 208 p.

A practical guide for industrial marketing research that explains objectives, functions, processes, practices, and applications. Management needs for current and projected information on markets, customers, end users, competitors, new products, and business trends are covered. The organization, recruitment, and training of the market research staff are included.

360. Platzer, Linda Cardillo. *Managing National Accounts.* New York: Conference Board, 1984. 35 p.

Successful busines-to-business marketing depends on developing a long-term relationship with the customer. The organizational and procedural approaches of various national account programs and the factors for success are covered, including charts, exhibits, and company examples.

361. Rawnsley, Allen, ed. *Manual of Industrial Marketing Research.* New York: Wiley, 1979. 196 p.

This manual covers planning, use of published information, surveys, forecasting, presentation of results, intelligence aspects of industrial marketing research, and the role of research in marketing and company planning.

362. Rexroad, Robert A. *High Technology Management.* New York: Wiley, 1983. 219 p.

For the company interested in marketing to industry or the government, this book provides information on topics such as company strategy and planning, competition and market analysis, forecasting, risk management, contracts, pricing, security, and communications.

363. Ross, Stewart Halsey. *The Management of Business-to-Business Advertising: A Working Guide for Small to Mid-Size Companies.* Westport, CT: Greenwood Press, 1986. 157 p.

This comprehensive, working guide for the industrial advertiser stresses practice rather than theory, covering the unique needs of a marketing-communication program for the industrial seller. Sales literature, direct mail, publicity, and trade shows are discussed. Developing an in-house advertising department, along with detailed instructions for organizing such a department are also included.

364. Stumm, David Arthur. *Advanced Industrial Selling.* New York: AMACOM, 1981. 221 p.

This book goes beyond the basic elements of selling and concentrates on strategies that demand knowledge of the product, industry, customer, and psychological behavior. It is aimed at salespeople who sell to professional industrial buyers. The case studies that are used demonstrate areas such as competitive selling techniques, negotiating skills, and concept selling.

PAPERS—COLLECTED

365. Hlavacek, James D., et al. *Industrial Marketing Perspectives: A Reader.* Chicago: American Marketing Assn., 1981. 237 p.
A collection of previously published journal articles of interest to practitioners and academics. The articles provide information and guidelines for effective marketing planning, research and decisions, and the dynamics of industrial promotion.

PERIODICALS/ANNUALS

366. *B/BCM: The Business-to-Business Catalog Marketer.* Biweekly. Colorado Springs, CO: Maxwell Sroge Publishing, Inc.
New ideas, answers concerning catalog or mail order business, techniques, advice, new developments, and successful ventures are some of the areas covered in this newsletter

367. *Business Marketing.* Monthly. Chicago: Crain Communications, Inc.
This business-to-business marketing magazine includes news and articles on strategy and tactics and has an annual listing of business/industrial advertising agencies. A monthly column, "Marketing Information," lists new marketing studies and directories.

368. *Customer Service Newsletter.* Monthly. Washington, DC: Marketing Publications, Inc.
Articles are about customer service that is provided by business to business, covering areas such as order processing, fulfillment, telephone use, controlling costs, government regulations, staff training, and trends.

369. *Industrial Distribution: For Industrial Distributors and Their Sales Personnel.* Monthly. New York: Technical Publishing.
A trade magazine covering topics such as industry and company news, sales and managment techniques, new products, and the quarterly inflation index. The annual survey of distributor operations has data on profit, loss, costs, inventory, trends, personnel, and computer usage.

370. *Industrial Marketing Management: The International Journal of Industrial Marketing and Marketing Research.* Quarterly. New York: Elsevier North-Holland Publishing Co., Inc.
Aimed at business people and scholars, this periodical focuses on buyer behavior, marketing research, marketing theory and applications, sales, and product management. Articles provide guidelines, techniques, and suggestions for problem solving.

371. *The Journal of Business & Industrial Marketing.* Quarterly. Santa Barbara, CA: Grayson Associates.
A publication for professional marketers and academicians that includes articles on research, cases, concepts, industry reviews, and practices that can be utilized in business practices.

372. *Survey of Industrial & Commercial Buying Power.* Annual. New York: Sales & Marketing Management.
The data cover shipments/receipts at the county level. The survey profiles each state and the top fifty manufacturing industries. The service industries of finance, health care, transportation, and wholesale trade are also included. This information is also in the April issue of *Sales & Marketing Management.*

373. Woodside, Arch G., ed. *Advances in Business Marketing: A Research Annual.* Annual. Greenwich, CT: JAI Press, Inc.

This annual illustrates the increasing attention business marketing is receiving as a theoretical and applied research topic. The lengthy empirical and theoretical, scholarly, research papers and literature reviews cover a variety of issues in industrial and commercial marketing.

PROCEEDINGS

374. *Seminar on Industrial Marketing Research: Developments Affecting Our Future.* Amsterdam, The Netherlands: European Society for Opinion and Marketing Research, 1981. 283 p.

The papers from this seminar, which was held in Budapest, Hungary, October 14-17, 1981, cover five broad areas—trends and prospects for industrial market research, development of new products, from research methodology to use in marketing, benefits to consumers from industrial marketing research, and international communication.

375. Spekman, Robert E., and Wilson, David T., eds. *Issues in Industrial Marketing: A View to the Future.* Chicago: American Marketing Assn., 1982. 99 p.

In an attempt to bridge the gap between marketing theory and marketing practice in industrial marketing, this collection of papers identifies areas needing additional research.

376. Spekman, Robert E., and Wilson, David T., eds. *A Strategic Approach to Business Marketing.* Chicago: American Marketing Assn., 1985. 193 p.

The papers cover topics such as competitive structures, application of market segmentation, market research in industrial organization, allocating R&D resources, and business marketing communications.

ASSOCIATIONS

Association of Industrial Advertisers. 41 E. 42nd St., New York, NY 10036.

Manufacturers Agents National Association. P.O. Box 3467, 23016 Mill Creek Rd., Laguna Hills, CA 92654.

Society of Manufacturers Representatives. 700 E. Maple Rd., No. 202, Birmingham, MI 48011.

United Association of Manufacturers Representatives. P.O. Drawer 6266, Kansas City, KS 66106.

SELLING TO GOVERNMENTS

Directories

377. Holtz, Herman. *Directory of Federal Purchasing Offices: Where, What, How to Sell to the U.S. Government.* New York: Wiley, 1981. 415 p.

Anyone interested in selling to the federal government will find this directory an excellent source of information. In addition to agency addresses, an explanation of the procurement system and an indication of what is purchased by each procurement office is included. A glossary of terms and an index by products and services is also provided.

Guidebooks/Handbooks

378. Cohen, William A. *How to Sell to the Government: A Step-by-Step Guide to Success.* New York: Wiley: 1981. 434 p.
Successful marketing to the federal government requires an understanding of the laws, regulation, rules, practices, procedures, or traditions that govern the purchasing process. This book covers a wide range of topics including the way the government does business, proposal writing, pricing, types of government contracts, and negotiations.

379. *A Guide to Doing Business with the Department of State.* Washington, DC: U.S. Government Printing Office, 1987. Various paging.
This guide for the small, minority- or female-owned business contains information on the State Department's procurement program including contract and subcontract opportunities, contacts for trade and investment issues, and a description of acquisition activities.

380. Holtz, Herman. *How to Sell Computer Services to Government Agencies.* New York; London: Chapman and Hall, 1985. 252 p.
The need for computers in government agencies is growing rapidly, and this book provides basic information for the company interested in this market. Information covering federal, state, and local governments includes bids and proposals, persuasive writing, R&D opportunities, and marketing research. Directories of federal, state, and local government prospects are included.

381. Holtz, Herman. *The $100 Billion Market: How to Do Business with the U.S. Government.* New York: AMACOM, 1982. 272 p.
This book focuses on federal contracts and the federal acquistion process noting the diversity of products and services purchased by the federal government. Understanding the system, locating government needs, making bids, determining costs, and writing proposals are some areas covered.

382. Holtz, Herman, and Schmidt, Terry. *The Winning Proposal: How to Write It.* New York: McGraw-Hill, 1981. 381 p.
Proposal writing ability is essential for any company seriously pursuing governmental business. This book provides guidance in techniques and methods for writing winning proposals for federal, state, and local governments. Information covered are types of contracts, statement of work, committee evaluations, common failures, proposal elements and formats, management plans, presentation strategies, and unsolicited proposals. A specimen proposal is included.

383. *How to Sell to Government Agencies.* Washington, DC: U.S. Government Printing Office, 1985. 8 p. (Subject Bibliography: SB-171)
This list of government publications includes sources that cover regulations, contracts, specificiations, and directory information necessary for anyone interested in selling to federal government agencies.

384. *Introduction to the Government Market: Local, State and Federal.* Cleveland, OH: Government Product News, 1983. 25 p.
How-to information that can help a business begin selling to any level of government includes a definition of the markets; steps for selling; product needs; particulars on local, state, and federal government selling; and a list of information sources.

385. Rexroad, Robert A. *Technical Marketing to the Government.* Chicago: Dartnell Corp., 1981. 263 p.

This manual, intended for the technical marketer, includes market planning aspects, bidding proposals, product support, and collecting marketing data. Specific information on the various branches of government buying agencies and their relationshop with industry is also covered.

386. Robertson, Jack C. *Selling to the Federal Government.* New York: McGraw-Hill, 1979. 234 p.

Anyone wanting to sell to the federal government should have knowledge of the Request for Proposal (RFP). This book covers RFP from conception to ultimate contract. Information covers the types of contracts, types of bids and bidding, pricing strategies, negotiations, evaluation boards, paper-work audits, and contract cancellations.

387. Seldon, M. Robert. *Life Cycle Costing: A Better Method of Government Procurement.* Boulder, CO: Westview Press, 1979. 283 p.

Life cycle costing includes total cost of product development procurement and ownership recognizing that the purchase price may be less significant than ownership costs. This book shows how government procurement agencies and industrial contractors can use this system effectively, explaining cost models and computer methods for selection of alternative procurements, the effective applications of these methods to optimize the life cycle cost of a project and a discussion of strategies needed to obtain the lowest life cycle costs.

388. *Selling to the Military; Army, Navy, Air Force, Defense Logistics Agency, Other Defense Agencies: General Information, Items Purchased, Location of Military Purchasing Offices.* Washington, DC: Department of Defense. U.S. Government Printing Office, 1987. 159 p.

Companies can use this guide to locate sales opportunities within the Department of Defense. The explanation of the military procurement process also includes copies of some necessary forms.

389. Speser, Philip; Drown, Jane Davis; and Drown, Clifford, eds. *The Defense-Space Market: A How-To Guide for Small Business.* New York: Frost & Sullivan, Inc., 1986. 307 p.

For the small business, this handbook provides guidance in marketing to defense and aerospace contractors, and to the Department of Defense and its prime contractors, NASA, the Department of Energy, and the Department of Transportation. The book applies marketing concepts to these industries and organizations and provides an overview of these specialized markets.

390. U.S. Small Business Administration. *U.S. Government Purchasing and Sales Directory: Guide for Selling and Buying in the Government Market.* Office of Procurement and Technical Assistance, Washington, DC: U.S. Government Printing Office, 1985. 191 p.

An alphabetical list of products and services purchased by civilian agencies and military departments. Explanations of assistance in obtaining prime contracts and subcontracts, and the market for research and development are included.

391. *Women Business Owners: Selling to the Federal Government.* Washington, DC: Interagency Committee on Woman's Business Enterprise, Office of Women's Business Ownership, U.S. Small Business Administration, 1987. 66 p.

Information on how the government buys and how to get on a bidder's list is covered. Also includes standard forms for bidding, purchasing, and generally doing business with the federal government. Sources of information and contact people are listed.

Periodicals

392. *Commerce Business Daily.* Daily. Washington, DC: U.S. Department of Commerce.

A Monday through Friday publication that lists U.S. government procurement invitations for services and supplies, contract awards, subcontracting leads, surplus property sales, and foreign business opportunities. Detailed descriptions of each item includes the contact person.

393. *Federal Contracts Report.* Loose-leaf with periodic updates. Washington, DC: Bureau of National Affairs, Inc. 2 vols.

Weekly updates provide the latest information about policies, procedures, and problems concerning government contracts covering topics such as minority contracting and subcontracting, competitive contracting, R&D procedures, congressional budget actions, major procurement agency meetings, and comment period deadlines.

394. *Government Contracts Report.* Loose-leaf with periodic updates. Chicago: Commerce Clearing House. 9 vols.

The periodic updates provide current information on laws and regulations affecting government contracts. Official texts and cases are organized by topics of the government's official procurement rules.

Associations

Coalition for Common Sense in Government Procurement. 1990 M St., N.W., Suite 400, Washington, DC 20036.

National Association of State Purchasing Officials. P.O. Box 11910, Lexington, KY 40578.

National Contract Management Assn. 6728 Old McLean Village Drive, McLean, VA 22101.

National Institute of Government Purchasing. 115 Hillwood Ave., Falls Church, VA 22046.

Consumer Behavior

BIBLIOGRAPHIES

395. Byerly, Greg, and Rubin, Richard E. *The Baby Boom: A Selective Annotated Bibliography.* Lexington, MA: Lexington Books, 1985. 238 p.

Books, dissertations, government publications, and journal articles over demographics, economic, sociological, and psychological marketing perspectives concerning this demographic phenomenon.

GUIDEBOOKS/HANDBOOKS

396. Britt, Steuart Henderson. *Psychological Principles of Marketing and Consumer Behavior.* Lexington, MA: Lexington Books, 1978. 532 p.

Almost 200 psychological principles of communication that are the result of research can be used to benefit business firms and consumers. These psychological principles can be applied to consumer behavior as the consumer is exposed to, perceives or learns about, is motivated or persuaded by products, packages, retailing, advertising, selling, and other aspects of marketing.

397. Greene, Jerome D. *Intelligent Marketers Guide to Consumer Models.* New York: Praeger, 1981. 170 p.

For marketing managers and researchers the mathematical models of population characteristics are explained concentrating on the logic, purpose, and results rather than on the formulas themselves.

398. Moschis, George P. *Consumer Socialization: A Life-Cycle Perspective.* Lexington MA: Lexington Books, 1987. 353 p.

Understanding the nature of changes in consumer behavior is important for those interested in marketing. The nature of these changes, how and why they occur, is covered in this book. The topics include models of consumer socialization and family, peers, mass media, socioeconomic, and racial influences, and the effects of age, life cycle, gender, and birth order.

399. O'Shaughnessy, John. *Why People Buy.* New York: Oxford University Press, 1987. 195 p.

This book is based on the interpretive social science approach that means recording what consumers say before they buy, during buying, and after buying and then interpreting the statements. From this the author derived six categories of consumer choice criteria that are subjective and objective. These can be used as a basis for developing a marketing strategy in relation to consumer motivations.

400. Schultz, Howard G.; Baird, Pamela C.; and Hawkes, Glenn R. *Lifestyles and Consumer Behavior of Older Americans.* New York: Praeger, 1979. 276 p.

Lifestyle patterns are related to consumer behavior in areas such as buying style, store choice, income management, food, housing, and clothes. Understanding these lifestyle differences among aging individuals has implications for the use of goods and services.

401. Settle, Robert B., and Alreck, Pamela L. *Why They Buy: American Consumers Inside and Out.* New York: Wiley, 1985. 351 p.

The forces shaping consumer buying decisions are outlined in this guide which includes information on social roles, affiliations, demographics, social class, and life stages. These are important to the marketer when identifying target market segments, planning the product or service mix, advertising, pricing, the communications, and the strategies. Examples of companies using these concepts are included.

402. Worcester, Robert M., and Downham, John, eds. *Consumer Market Research Handbook.* 3d rev. ed. New York: North-Holland, 1986. 840 p.

The techniques of market research, including areas such as sampling, questionnaire design, panel research, statistics, and significance testing are included in this book. The use of marketing research discusses segmenting and constructing markets, new product development, packaging research, market modeling, print media research.

MINORITY/ETHNIC CONSUMERS

403. Guernica, Antonio. *Reaching the Hispanic Market Effectively: The Media, the Market, the Methods.* New York: McGraw-Hill, 1982. 189 p.

Use of the Spanish language defines the Hispanic market and the in-depth view of Spanish media, and an overview of the target audience covers Spanish print, radio, and television. An extensive demographic profile and the guidelines for planning and strategy for use of the media is also covered.

404. *The Hispanic Almanac.* Washington, DC: Hispanic Policy Development Project, 1984. 164 p.

The socioeconomic data for various Hispanic groups covers age, sex distribution, income, employment, and education status. The top twenty Hispanic market profiles present information on the size and growth potential, and the Area of Dominent Influence (ADI).

405. *Minority Marketing.* Chicago: Crain Books, 1980. 88 p.

A reprint of material in *Advertising Age/Section 2,* a center pullout of this magazine, that covered minority marketing techniques and strategies for the black, Hispanic, and Jewish populations.

406. Spencer, Gregory. *Projections of the Hispanic Population: 1983 to 2080.* Washington, DC: Bureau of the Census, 1986. 85 p. (Current Population Reports, Series P-25, no 995).

Projections by age and sex are based on three levels of fertility, mortality, and net immigration trends. Included is information on areas such as projected percent of change, median age, number of dependents, and components of change for the United States as a whole.

PERIODICALS/ANNUALS

407. *Journal of Consumer Marketing.* Quarterly. Santa Barbara, CA: Grayson Associates.

Articles aimed at the marketing practitioner are concerned with new ideas applicable to marketing situations. The basis may be research or case studies of buyer behavior, marketing research, management, and marketing theory.

408. *Journal of Consumer Research: An Interdisciplinary Quarterly.* Quarterly. Los Angeles: Journal of Consumer Research, Inc.

Nearly a dozen scholarly associations sponsor this journal. The articles are interdisciplinary empirical research on consumer behavior related to the purchase of goods or services, processes that lead to the purchase, including advertising.

409. Sheth, Jagdish N., ed. *Research in Consumer Behavior.* Annual. Greenwich, CT: JAI Press, Inc.

Scholarly and state-of-the art papers on consumer behavior are included in this series which is intended for monographic length papers that are too long for journal articles.

PROCEEDINGS

410. *Advances in Consumer Research.* Annual. Provo, UT: Association for Consumer Research, Graduate School of Management, Brigham Young University.

Papers presented at the annual conference cover theoretical, methodological, and empirical research for all areas of consumer information.

411. Olson, Jerry, and Sentis, Keith. *Advertising and Consumer Psychology.* Vol 3. New York: Praeger, 1986. 294 p.

The papers presented at the Advertising and Consumer Psychology Conference, held in June 1984 in New York, sponsored by Ted Bates Advertising, the Marketing Science Institute, and Division 23 of the American Psychological Association cover topics such as nonverbal measurement of consumers' responses, consumers' evaluation of advertising, the role of self concerning advertising effects, and the measurement of consumers' meanings for advertising.

STATISTICAL INFORMATION

412. *Consumer Attitudes and Buying Plans.* Monthly. New York: Conference Board.

Indexes of consumer confidence and buying plans that cover more than ten years are graphically presented in this publication. Statistical data, based on consumer surveys, includes information on expectations for business conditions and intentions for purchase by month, for the period of a year.

413. *Consumer Market Developments.* Annual. New York: Fairchild Publications.

A special report of the *Fairchild Fact File* that has demographic and economic data on consumer market conditions for various periods from 1970 to 2000. Most data are from the U.S. Census Bureau or the U.S. Bureau of Labor Statistics and cover population, vital statistics, household, labor force, earnings, housing, personal expenditures, and other related data.

414. *Consumer Market Guide.* Loose-leaf. New York: Consumer Research Center, The Conferenc Board.

This loose-leaf publication is an up-dated and comprehensive statistical collection of data on a variety of demographic and socioeconomic statistics including expenditures, retailing, advertising, prices, and production. These data are based on the Census Bureau's demographic file which comes from the March publication of *Current Population Survey.*

415. *The Survey of Buying Power Data Service.* Annual. New York: Sales & Marketing Management.

Included in this loose-leaf compilation of demographic, economic, and sales data are detailed population characteristics, household income, buying income, retail sales by twelve store groups, ten merchandise lines, market data, and metropolitan/county market projections for population, income, and retail sales. The information is organized by geographic region, state, metropolitan area, county, and TV market area, with summary and ranking tables.

416. *Survey of Buying Power. Part I.* Annual. New York: Sales & Marketing Management.

Part one, released annually in July, provides data on demographics, buying income; spending patterns; retail sales for major lines; and market indexes for metropolitan, city, county, and state markets. This is a separate publication for information appearing in the *Sales & Marketing Management* magazine.

417. *Survey of Buying Power. Part II.* Annual. New York: Sales & Marketing Management.

Published annually in October, this survey has detailed population, income, retail sales, and buying power data for television and newspaper markets in the U.S. and Canada. The television market indicates the Areas of Dominant Influence (ADI). Dominance and effective coverage is given for newspaper markets, projected five-year growth of population, income, and retail sales for U.S. metropolitan areas and states.

ASSOCIATIONS

American Association for Public Opinion Research. P.O. Box 17, Princeton, NJ 08540.

American Psychological Association. Division of Consumer Psychology, 1200 17th St., N.W., Washington, DC 20036.

Association for Consumer Research, Graduate School of Management. 632 TNRB, Brigham Young University, Provo, UT 84602.

National Association of Market Developers. P.O. Box 4560, Stamford, CT 06907.

Direct Marketing

BIBLIOGRAPHIES

418. Direct Selling Education Foundation. *A Selected Annotated Bibliography on Direct Selling in the United States.* Washington, DC: The Foundation, 1982. 50 p.

> Although there are some omissions in this bibliography, it provides a list of 364 items on direct (in-home) selling. Books, marketing texts, periodical articles, published from 1956 to 1982 are arranged alphabetically by author or title and are grouped by format. No subject index is provided.

DICTIONARIES

419. Bodian, Nat G. *Encyclopedia of Mailing List Terminology.* Winchester, MA: Bret Scot Press, 1986. 320 p.

> Definitions of mailing list terms and phrases cover acquiring, renting, compiling, evaluating, testing, and updating mailing lists. Appendices cover rules, trade customs, software capabilities, database participation, and a mailing list chronology.

DIRECTORIES

420. *Direct Mail List Rates and Data.* Monthly. Wilmette, IL: Standard Rate & Data Service.

> A directory of mailing list brokers, compilers, and managers, a classified listing of business direct mailing lists, co-op mailings, package inserts, and consumer and farm lists that are available for the direct mail industry.

421. Direct Marketing Assn. *Membership Roster.* Annual. New York.

> A full listing of all companies that are members of this association.

422. *The Direct Marketing Market Place: Including a Directory of Names, Addresses and Phone Numbers.* Annual. Hewlett Harbor, NY: Hilary House Publishers.

> Divided into three sections by products and services, firms and supplies, and creative services, each entry includes address, telephone number, key marketing executive names, and sales or revenue figures. Separate indexes of individuals and geographic locations are provided.

423. *Directory of Mailing List Houses: A Complete Guide to Mailing List Sources.* 10th ed. Coral Springs, FL: B. Klein Publications, 1987. 366 p.
The names of more than 2,000 mailing list specialists are listed geographically and by list specialities which includes list brokers, list compilers, and list management firms. Managers, telephone numbers, and other information needed to slect the right list company are included.

424. Gottlieb, Richard, ed. *The Directory of Mail Order Catalogs.* 3d ed. Sharon, CT: Grey House Publishing, 1987. 363 p.
More than 5,000 active, consumer mail order companies in the U.S. are listed in this catalog. The entries include executives, buyers, marketing managers, sales volume, product areas, catalog information, and type of merchandise sold.

425. Iglesia, Maria de la. *The Ultimate Shopper's Catalogue.* New York: Harper & Row, 1987. 355 p.
Although aimed at the shopper, the direct marketer can use this to learn about the competition. Organized by type of product, the chapters list the companies handling products such appliances, cars, fabrics, food, and furniture, including information on the frequency and cost of the company's catalog, forms of payment accepted, phone number, address, extent of products, and representative prices.

426. *Mail Order Business Directory: A Complete Guide to the Mail Order Market.* 14th ed. Coral Springs, FL: B. Klein Publications, 1986. 366 p.
Useful for manufacturers, this directory lists the names of the 9,000 most active mail order and catalog houses arranged by state. Each entry lists buyers and the lines carried by the company.

GUIDEBOOKS/HANDBOOKS

427. Bernstein, Ronald A. *Successful Direct Selling: How to Plan, Launch, Promote and Maintain a Profitable Direct-Selling Company.* Englewood Cliffs, NJ: Prentice-Hall, 1984. 220 p.
For the company that wants to branch out into direct selling, or the individual who wants to start such a business, this guide provides practical advice on planning, operational approaches, recruiting, training, sales promotion, and laws affecting direct selling. Case histories of successful direct selling companies are included.

428. Burns, Karen L., ed. *Guiding Catalog Growth: Successful Strategies, Management and Techniques.* New York: Direct Marketing Assn., Inc., 1985. 299 p.
Written by those active in the field, the areas covered include customer acquistion methods, market research, pricing, merchandise testing, improving fulfillment operations, catalog preparation and production, start-up budgeting, telemarketing services, and list segmentation.

429. Burstiner, Irving. *Mail Order Selling.* Englewood Cliffs, NJ: Prentice-Hall, 1982. 262 p.
For the beginner, this guidebook is a nontechnical approach to starting a mail order business. Techniques and helpful advice provide information on how to successfully operate such a business.

430. Cohen, William A. *Building a Mail Order Business: A Complete Manual for Success.* 2d ed. New York: Wiley, 1985. 495 p.
From basic to sophisticated methods for increasing sales are explained in detail showing step-by-step methods of how to do it. This covers the marketing plan, product selection, writing ads, graphics, competition, list ordering techniques, and copyright protection.

431. *Direct Mail Marketing Manual.* Loose-leaf. New York: Direct Mail/Marketing Assn. 2 vols.

Detailed information in these volumes covers direct marketing research, sales promotion, small business managment, new technology, media, and market applications. DMA references and a keyword index are provided. Updated every year by new releases.

432. *Fact Book: An Overview of Direct Marketing and Direct Response Advertising.* 9th ed. New York: Direct Marketing Assn., Inc., 1986. 220 p.

Information on lists, direct mail, catalogs, telemarketing, print advertising, new electonic media, business-to-business catalogs, consumer atttitudes, financial services, and fund raising are some of the areas covered in this edition. *Statistics and Market Data* is the supplement that contains data on media, markets, consumer demographics, and buying behavior.

433. Gosden, Freeman F., Jr. *Direct Marketing Success: What Works and Why.* New York: Wiley, 1986. 225 p.

The author explains why something is done, rather than just giving a how-to explanation. Because each marketing project is different, understanding the why makes it easier to adapt a technique to a new situation.

434. Graham, John W., and Jones, Susan K. *Selling by Mail: An Entrepreneurial Guide to Direct Marketing.* New York: Scribners, 1985. 309 p.

Written for the novice with no prior direct marketing experience, this book explains how to start an in-house direct marketing operation, covering selection of outside sources, evaluating, testing, budgeting, legal concerns, and planning. In the appendix are lists of direct marketing terms, books, periodicals, and associations.

435. Harper, Rose. *Mailing List Strategies: A Guide to Direct Mail Success.* New York: McGraw-Hill, 1986. 213 p.

The customer file is not only an important asset of direct mail marketing, but it is also a marketing decision support system. Because a constant development of new customers is necessary, this book covers information about list companies, renting lists, types of direct response lists, researching market potential, internal files, and list security.

436. Hodgson, Richard S. *The Dartnell Direct Mail and Mail Order Handbook.* 3d ed. Chicago: Dartnell Corp., 1980. 1,538 p.

A practical guide to developing a direct mail/mail order program that assists with planning, creating, and producing campaigns that are flexible and profitable. Checklists, reference data, successful ideas, testing for better results, sampling, couponing, merging, and purging mailing lists are a few of the areas covered.

437. Holtz, Herman. *Direct Marketer's Workbook.* New York: Wiley, 1986. 348 p.

A pracical handbook that explains how to develop a successful sales campaign through the mails that features worksheets and checklists to guide the marketer through product selection, concept development, market testing, production, order processing, and sales tracking.

438. King, Norman. *Big Sales from Small Spaces.* New York: Facts on File Publications, 1986. 192 p.

Techniques for effective small-space advertising in direct marketing cover types of ads, how they are used in newspapers and magazines, design of graphics, effective headlines and telegraphic copy, costs, where to advertise, and testing the ad.

439. Kobs, Jim. *Profitable Direct Marketing: How to Start, Improve or Expand Any Direct Marketing Operation.* Chicago: Crain Books, 1979. 328 p.

A guide to what one needs to know to launch a direct marketing business or to improve one, by learning how to select products and services and relate the offer to the business objective and the use of multimedia to obtain the best results. Problems and solutions in direct marketing are also covered.

440. Lumley, James E. A. *Sell It by Mail: Making Your Product the One They Buy.* New York: Wiley, 1986. 382 p.

A practical guide to direct marketing techniques in areas such as research, copy design, printing, developing marketing lists and learning what elicits a consumer's response. The step-by-step method includes key points and cautions.

441. Muldoon, Katie. *Catalog Marketing: The Complete Guide to Profitability in the Catalog Business.* New York: Bowker, 1984. 312 p.

A step-by-step explanation of how to produce effective consumer catalogs. Examples of successful catalogs, illustrations, and trade secrets provide information on maximizing sales while minimizing costs.

442. Nash, Edward L. *Direct Marketing: Strategy, Planning, Execution.* 2d ed. New York: McGraw-Hill, 1986. 445 p.

Direct marketing uses any media—mail, newspapers, magazines, radio, television, matchbook covers, telephone, mailgram—to reach the buyer. Practical informtion about the market plan, mailing lists, research, graphic design, economics, and even the future are covered.

443. Posch, Robert J. *Direct Marketer's Legal Advisor.* New York: McGraw-Hill, 1982. 256 p.

This book provides a discussion of the law and feasible solutions for potential problems in direct marketing. It is not a substitute for professional advice but provides an understanding of compliance issues such as pricing, free gifts, sweepstakes, discounting, and credit testing.

444. Simon, Julian L. *How to Start and Operate a Mail-Order Business.* 4th ed. New York: McGraw-Hill, 1987. 547 p.

A step-by-step approach to starting a mail order business that teaches the business as well as outlining the decisions that must be made. Facts and data about the business, products that sell, strategies, testing, advertising costs, and use of the computer are some of the areas covered.

445. Smith, Lou E. *How to Create Successful Catalogs.* Colorado Springs, CO: Maxwell Sroge Publising, Inc. 1985. 459 p.

Step-by-step guidelines cover planning, writing, designing, photographing, producing, and printing the successful catalog. Checklists, timetables, and glossary are included.

446. Sroge, Maxwell. *Inside the Leading Mail Order Houses.* 2d ed. Colorado Springs, CO: Maxwell Sroge Publishing, Inc., 1984. 538 p.

Technologies, techniques, and procedures that are used by successful mail order houses are covered. Product positioning decisions, mailing schedules, names and titles of major industry executives, new developments and products, facilities, acquisitions and new ventures, facts and figures are included.

447. Stone, Bob. *Successful Direct Marketing Methods.* 3d ed. Chicago: Crain Books, 1984. 496 p.

A practical book that has a sound conceptual base, covers areas such as direct marketing research, use of direct marketing in the marketing mix, and strategic business planning. Basics such as start-up procedures, selection of merchandise, choosing the media, and producing direct mail packages that work are thoroughly explained.

PERIODICALS

448. *AIS 800 Report.* Semimonthly. New York: Advertising Information Service.
For those using the toll-free marketing technique, this newsletter covers information on equipment, available services, and topics such as how to avoid costly mistakes and what works and what doesn't.

449. *The Catalog Marketer.* Biweekly. Colorado Spring, CO: Maxwell Sroge Publishing.
Practical information on the creation, production, and mailing of profitable catalogs is covered in this publication. Profit-generating strategies, tips for cutting costs, list maintenance, and chosing and pricing merchandise are a few of the areas included.

450. *DirecTech Report.* Monthly. Colorado Springs, CO: Maxwell Sroge Publishing.
For the direct marketing executive, this publication provides information on the use of electronic technology in direct marketing by analyzing what's happening and what works, reporting on research of possible applications and test results, explaining the mechanics of new technologies, and providing competitor information.

451. *Direct Line: The DMA Newsletter.* Monthly. New York: Direct Marketing Assn., Inc.
A newsletter for members of the association that has information on trends, technology, acquistions and mergers, research news, and case studies.

452. *Direct Marketing Magazine.* Monthly. Garden City, NY: Hoke Communications.
Included in this publication is information about the use of mailing lists, direct response advertising used by various businesses such as manufacturers, retailers, wholesalers, banks, and insurance companies and reports on the use of new technology with its impact on direct marketing.

453. *Direct Response: The Digest of Direct Marketing.* Bimonthly. Torrance, CA: Infomat, Inc.
The most important articles from advertising and business publications that are of interest to direct mail companies are summarized. Areas covered include media, graphics, testing, buying habits, laws and regulations, telemarketing, and computers.

454. *Directions.* Bimonthly. New York: Direct Marketing Assn.
This newsletter covers consumer attitudes and trends, direct marketing techniques, information on postal regulations, and ongoing research projects for the association. The former title was *Direct Marketing Journal.*

455. *DM News: The Newspaper of Direct Marketing.* Semimonthly. New York: Mill Hollow Corp.
This tabloid publication covers news and issues of interest to those associated with direct marketing. Included is information on new campaigns, agency and association news, regular columns by direct marketing experts, and special reports on telemarketing. The ads are a source for available mailing lists and software management packages for these lists.

456. *Mail Order Digest.* Monthly. Los Angeles: National Mail Order Assn.
This newsletter covers topics such as developments, promotional plan, new product sources, merchandising methods, sources for mailing lists, and business opportunities for mail order selling.

457. *Non-Store Marketing Report.* Biweekly. Colorado Springs, CO: Maxwell Sroge Publishing.
A newsletter that contains company profiles, case studies, a quarterly compilation of selected financial statistics, current trends, eight special reports that provide in-depth coverage of key industry segments, forecasts, and analysis of successful marketing techniques and innovations.

458. *Zip Target Marketing: The Magazine of Communications, Lists, Mailing, Fulfillment.* Monthly. Philadelphia, PA: North American Publishing Co.
Intended for the direct mail executive, the focus is on articles discussing the use of direct mail and telemarketing techniques.

STATISTICAL INFORMATION

459. *All about Mail Order; Facts, Trends, Key Data.* Annual. Colorado Springs, CO: Maxwell Sroge Publishing.
This review of mail order marketing in the U.S. and abroad covers sales and marketing analysis for consumer and business/industrial mail order. In addition, data on socioeconomic trends and marketplace technologies are covered.

460. *Apparel-by-Mail Industry Data Reports.* Annual. Colorado Springs, CO: Maxwell Sroge Publishing.
There are five reports that provide a comprehensive and in-depth look at this industry: *Profiles of Leading Apparel-by-Mail Companies, Directory of 600 Apparel-by-Mail Companies, Industry Structure and Segmentation, Marketing/Merchandising/ Creative Strategies,* and *Catalog Space Allocation Tables.*

461. *Food-by-Mail Industry Data Reports.* Annual. Colorado Springs, CO: Maxwell Sroge Publishing.
The following reports give a comprehensive and in-depth look at this industry: *Executive Summary, Profiles of Leading Food-by-Mail Companies, Industry Structure and Segmentation, Merchandising/Marketing/Operations, Outlooks/Trends, Catalog Space Allocation Tables, Special Segments (Cheese & Gift, Fruit, Dessert, Meat, Nuts, Kitchenware).*

462. *Mail Order Data.* Annual. Colorado Springs, CO: Maxwell Sroge Publishing.
Although this is the new title for *All about Mail Order,* the same type of information is included. Mail order marketing in the U.S. and abroad covers thirty-one product areas including information on sales and marketing analysis, socioeconomic and buying trends, and mail order opportunities for consumer and industrial companies.

463. *Supplement to the Fact Book: Statistics and Market Data.* Biannual. New York: Direct Marketing Assn., Inc.
This is a supplement to the *Fact Book: An Overview of Direct Marketing and Direct Response Advertising.* The publication has graphs and charts on media, markets, consumer demographics, buying behavior, and other data.

ASSOCIATIONS

Associated Third Class Mail Users. 1725 K St., N.W., Washington, DC 20006.

Association of Direct Marketing Agencies. 342 Madison Ave., Suite 1818, New York, NY 10017.

Direct Mail/Marketing Assn. 6 East 43rd St., New York, NY 10017.

Direct Marketing Creative Guild, Inc. 516 Fifth Ave., New York, NY 10036.

Direct Marketing Educational Foundation. 6 East 43rd St., New York: NY 10017.

Direct Selling Assn. 1730 M St., N.W., Suite 610, Washington, DC 20036.

Fulfillment Management Assn. 755 Second Ave., New York, NY 10017.

National Mail Order Assn. 5818 Venice Blvd., Los Angeles, CA 90019.

Third Class Mail Assn. 1122 15th St., N.W., Suite 1037, Washington, DC 20005.

Women's Direct Response Group. P.O. Box 1561, FDR Station, New York, NY 10150.

TELEMARKETING

Directory

464. *NATA Telecommunications Sourcebook.* Annual. Washington, DC: North American Telephone Assn.
> For telemarketers, this source book provides information on areas such as equipment, software, periodicals, and trade shows.

Guidebooks/Handbooks

465. Fisher, Peg. *Successful Telemarketing: A Step-by-Step Guide for Increased Sales at Lower Cost.* Chicago: Dartnell Corp., 1985. 300 p.
> The proven potential of telemarketing is covered in this loose-leaf guidebook to the techniques that can assist the sales manager in maximizing profits at a minimum of cost. The basics are covered with clear explanations for the person new to this method of marketing.

466. Jordan, Alan. *The Only Telemarketing Book You'll Ever Need.* 2d ed. Wayne, PA: Add-Effect Associates, Inc., 1983. 222 p.
> This manual gives practical advice for developing qualified leads, converting phone inquiries into sales, and closing over the phone. Sample forms of data collection, sample phrases to be used as models, discussion of the use of 800 numbers and WATS lines, and nontechnical explanations of sequencers and automatic call distributors are some of the areas covered.

467. Kordahl, Eugene G. *Telemarketing for Business: A Guide to Building Your Own Telemarketing Operation.* Englewood Cliffs, NJ: Prentice-Hall, 1984. 324 p.
> The author developed telephone marketing programs for many leading U.S. companies, and this book explains the techniques that will increase sales per customer,

lower sales costs, improve customer service, and increase new product and market penetration.

468. Masser, Barry Z., and Leeds, William M. *Power-Selling by Telephone.* West Nyack, NY: Parket Publishing Co., Inc., 1982. 240 p.
Structured techniques that are modular and easy to learn provide an effective telephone selling system. This book includes checklists, step-by-step instructions for custom tailoring a total delivery system, evaluating techniques, setting quotas, and monitoring follow-up procedures.

469. McCafferty, Thomas. *In-House Telemarketing: A Masterplan for Starting and Managing a Profitable Telemarketing Program.* Chicago: Probus Publishing Co., 1987. 337 p.
A guide to planning and implementing a telemarketing program that can either support traditional marketing approaches or provide advantages over traditional methods. It also identifies the marketing challenges particularly applicable to telemarketing. Forms, checklists, and sources of information are included.

470. Ortland, Gerald. *Telemarketing: High-Profit Telephone Selling Techniques.* Loose-leaf. New York: Wiley, 1982. 190 p.
A self-paced, practical guide explains how to set up and manage a telephone selling program and incorporate it in the marketing plan. Checksheets are also included.

471. Osborne, G. Scott. *Electronic Direct Marketing.* Englewood Cliffs, NJ: Prentice-Hall, 1984. 163 p.
The marketing opportunities using electronic media, including television, radio, the telephone, and other electronic technologies, are covered. These electronic direct marketing techniques are becoming increasingly important, even to small businesses.

472. Roman, Murray. *Telemarketing Campaigns That Work!* Englewood Cliffs, NJ: Prentice-Hall, 1983. 274 p.
Practical advice on the use of telephone marketing campaigns for direct marketing to consumers or business-to-business marketing is given in this publications.

473. Stone, Bob, and Wyman, John. *Successful Telemarketing: Opportunities and Techniques for Increasing Sales and Profits.* Englewood Cliffs, NJ: Prentice-Hall, 1986. 236 p.
A practical guide for developing a successful telemarketing program that shows how to reduce costs, develop inexpensive commercials, target campaigns to customer needs, provide customized service, and implement a customer database.

474. Strauss, Lawrence. *Electronic Marketing: Emerging TV and Computer Channels for Interactive Home Shopping.* White Plains, NY: Knowledge Industry Publications, Inc., 1983. 141 p.
The elements necessary for developing electronic marketing are examined in this book. These include the communications support structure, relation between direct marketing and technology, consumer acceptance, role of advertising, and economic and social conditions.

475. *Telemarketing's 100 Do's and Don'ts.* Norwalk, CT: Technology Marketing Corp., 1986. 141 p.
This professional guide, compiled by the editorial staff of *Telemarketing* magazine, provides information on how to avoid costly mistakes. Planning, recruiting, and training; acquiring equipment; developing a data support system; and list selection are some areas covered. A list of telemarketing and communication terms are included.

476. Weitzen, H. Skip. *Telephone Magic: How to Tap the Phone's Marketing Potential in Your Business.* New York: McGraw-Hill, 1987. 192 p.

The use of telephone technologies by business, entrepreneurs, service, and nonprofit organizations can create cost-effective and profitable ways of reaching customers. Techniques covered include extension of advertising capabilities, prospecting, reduction of sales costs, research, use of new telephone products, and pricing.

Periodicals

477. *Telemarketing: The Magazine of Business Telecommunication.* Monthly. Norwalk, CT: Technology Marketing Corp.

A how-to approach to telemarketing that covers systems, regulations, use of telemarketing in various industries and bridges the gap between telecommunication suppliers and end users. An annual listing of the top fifty service bureaus is also included.

Associations

American Telemarketing Assn. 1800 Pickwick Ave., Glenview, IL 60025.

Franchising

GUIDEBOOKS/HANDBOOKS

478. Bond, Robert E. *The Source Book of Franchise Opportunities.* Homewood, IL: Dow Jones-Irwin, 1985. 509 p.

The purpose of this book is to provide assistance in deciding which franchise meets an individual's needs, experience level, and financial position. The franchises are arranged in forty-four categories. Comparable information about the 1,400 listings includes financial data, services of the company, and a brief explanation of the organization. An index by category and an alphabetical listing are included.

479. *Franchise Annual: Complete Handbook and Directory.* Annual. New York: Information Press, Inc.

More than 3,000 franchises, including American, Canadian, and overseas listings, are presented along with information for the potential franchisee. Categorical and alphabetical indexes are provided.

480. *Franchise Opportunities Handbook.* Annual. Washington, DC: U.S. Department of Commerce, International Trade Administration and Minority Business Development Agency. U.S Government Printing Office.

The introductory section contains general information, on franchising, checklists, and other sources of information. The franchises are listed alphabetically including description, number in operation, equity needed, financial assistance available, training, and managerial assistance. A category index is provided.

481. Seltz, David D. *The Complete Handbook of Franchising.* Reading MA: Addison-Wesley, 1982. 247 p.

Franchising guidelines, information, and data are presented along with forms, charts, and agreements to aid in business development. Some topics included are allotment, financing, personnel, promotion, and need for an operations manual.

482. Smith, Brian R., and West, Thomas L. *Buying a Franchise.* Lexington, MA: Stephen Greene, 1986. 100 p.

A useful, detailed guide that describes the franchise market, its opportunities, legal consideration, and negotiations with franchisors. Checklists provide a measurement of management skills and suitability of opportunities. Case studies, financial tables, and bibliographic references are included.

483. Tarbutton, Lloyd T. *Franchising: The How-To Book.* Englewood Cliffs, NJ: Prentice-Hall, 1986. 226 p.

For the individual interested in franchising, information on all aspects of this type of business relationship is supplied including what a franchise is, what is purchased, design of the operation, capital needs, long-range planning, consultants, laws and regulation, contracts, and all aspects of operating such a business.

484. Webster, Bryce. *The Insider's Guide to Franchising.* New York: AMACOM/American Management Assn., 1986. 309 p.

Specific, practical advice is given for anyone contemplating buying a franchise. Deciding the best franchise for you includes evaluation opportunities, negotiating a contract, start-up costs, financing, hiring and training workers, marketing and promotion, expansion, and relations with the franchisor.

PERIODICALS/ANNUALS

485. *Franchising World.* Quarterly. Washington, DC: International Franchise Assn.

Current information on franchising covers trends, developments, operations, management, public relations, and interviews with franchisors.

486. U.S. Bureau of Domestic Commerce. *Franchising in the Economy.* Annual. Washington, DC: U.S. Government Printing Office.

The first section is an explanation of the survey results covering trends, outlook, company characteristics, minotiry franchisees and dominant types of franchises. The tables and charts, which are more than half of the publication, have data on sales, number of establishments, rankings by type of franchise, and information on specific franchises.

ASSOCIATIONS

American Franchise Assn. 12077 Wilshire Blvd., Suite 750, Los Angeles, CA 90025.

International Franchise Assn. 1025 Connecticut Ave., N.W., Suite 707, Washington, DC 20036.

New Products

BIBLIOGRAPHIES

487. Balachandran, Sarojini, ed. *New Product Planning: A Guide to Information Sources.* Detroit, MI: Gale Research, 1980. 231 p.

An annotated bibliography of journal articles, books, proceedings, reports, case studies, and histories that is arranged by major subject headings. The material is generally limited to the 1970s.

488. Hill, Conrad R. *Trademarks and Brand Management: Selected Annotations.* New York: United States Trademark Assn., 1976. 188 p.

Although dated, this bibliography of journal articles and books is a starting point. No index is provided, but the detailed table of contents lists topics such as trademark selection, development, management, legal aspects, international trademarks, consumer behavior, brand management, and promotion.

489. Rothberg, Robert R., and Mellott, Douglas W., comps. *New Product Planning: Management of the Marketing/R&D Interface: An Annotated Bibliography.* Chicago: American Marketing Assn., 1977. 44 p.

This bibliography, intended for the practitioner and the academician, addresses the communication and authority issues concerning the interface between the marketing and the R&D departments. The journal articles were published prior to 1976 and cover areas such as the importance of innovation, strategy and planning, organization and integration, concept generation, and evaluation.

DATABASES

Patent information is divided into seven databases covering various types of citations. See one of the database directories listed in the chapter Marketing—General Information for a complete listing. The databases listed below cover basic information.

490. Claims/Citation. Coverage varies. Alexandria, VA: IFI/Plenum Data Co. (Vendor: DIAL)

Provides access to every U.S. and non-U.S. patent, a listing of over 12,000,000 patent numbers. Each record lists the patent number of each later patent that cites it. The cited patents are 1836 to date, the citing patents are 1947 to date.

491. PTS New Product Announcements. 1985–. Cleveland, OH: Predicasts, Inc. (Vendors: BRS, DIAL)
The announcements are full-text press releases that cover new products and services and include information on price, specifications, new technologies, distribution channels, and availability.

492. Thomas New Industrial Products. 1984–. New York: Thomas Publishing Co., Inc. (Vendor: DIAL)
Provides infromation on new industrial products and systems taken from product press releases of manufacturers and distributors.

493. Trademarkscan. 1984–. North Quincy, MA: Thomson & Thomson. (Vendor: DIAL)
The database provides a rapid scan of more than 1,000,000 currently active trademarks registered in the U.S. Patent and Trademark Office.

494. Trademarkscan State. 1986–. North Quincy, MA: Thomson & Thomson. (Vendor: DIAL)
Information on trademarks registered in the fifty states and Puerto Rico are included for every type of product or service marketed commercially.

495. World Patents Index. 1980–. London: Derwent Publications, Ltd. (Vendor: DIAL)
The file contains data on almost 3,000,000 inventions in more than 6,000,000 documents from thrity patent issuing authorities in the world.

DIRECTORIES

496. Frankenstein, Diane Waxer, and Frankenstein, George. *Brandnames: Who Owns What*. New York: Facts on File, 1986. 457 p.
This guide lists the company that ultimately owns a product name. For the more than 7,900 major consumer corporations, each entry has a brief corporate history and a list of brand names. Also included are the largest foreign companies selling in the U.S. A list of product categories and a detailed index are provided.

497. Kuwayama, Yasaburo. *Trademarks and Symbols*. New York: Van Nostrand Reinhold Co., 1973. 2 vols. 192 p.; 186 p.
An illustrated guide to more than 1,300 worldwide trademarks covering all type of industries and designs. Volume one is arranged alphabetically; volume two is arranged by symbol or design.

498. Morgan, Hal. *Symbols of America*. New York: Viking, 1986. 239 p.
The selected designs in this book have historic and artistic merit and represent the best known trademarks from a wide variety of industries. These marks are used to promote recognition and the individuality of a product or company.

499. *Trademark Register of the United States*. Annual. Washington, DC: Patent Searching Service.
Currently in force and renewed trademarks registered in the U.S. Patent and Trademark Office are arranged by International Classification Schedule numbers for goods, products, and services. Expired registrations are not included.

500. Wood, Donna, ed. *Trade Names Dictionary.* 5th ed. Detroit, MI: Gale Research Co., 1986. 2 vols. 1,828 p.

Trade, brand, product, design, and coined names are alphabetically listed. Each entry gives the name, product description, company distributor's name, and a code to the sources for this information. A supplement, *New Trade Names,* provides a list of new trade names and company names.

501. Wood, Donna, ed. *Trade Names Dictionary: Company Index.* 5th ed. Detroit, MI: Gale Research Co., 1986. 2 vols. 1,838 p.

A companion to the *Trade Names Dictionary,* this is an alphabetical name and address list of the 41,000 companies in the basic volumes. For each company the name of the product manufactured, marketed, or imported and a product description are included.

GUIDEBOOKS/HANDBOOKS

502. Bailey, Earl L., ed. *Product-Line Strategies.* New York: The Conference Board, 1982. 76 p.

The practical issues and options facing the company developing a marketing strategy for its products require a disciplined approach. The fundamental framework for product-line strategy is outlined, and the planning prospects and requirements for consumer products and industrial markets are presented separately.

503. Bobrow, Edwin E., and Shafer, Dennis W. *Pioneering New Products: A Market Survival Guide.* Homewood, IL: Dow Jones-Irwin, 1987. 234 p.

This is a practical, goal-oriented guide for marketers, entrepreneurs, and "intrapreneurs" that covers a systematic approach to new product development and marketing.

504. Cafarelli, Eugene J. *Developing New Products and Repositioning Mature Brands: A Risk-Reduction System That Produces Investment Alternatives.* New York: Wiley, 1980. 253 p.

For both the market practitioner and the general management person, this step-by-step procedure explains specific objectives and the appropriate research or creativity tools needed to reduce the risk of new product introduction.

505. Choffray, Jean-Marie, and Lilien, Gary L. *Market Planning for New Industrial Products.* New York: Wiley, 1980. 294 p.

Written for professional managers and market researchers, this book is for the nontechnical reader. It covers ways to measure, analyze, and model response to industrial marketing strategy.

506. Cleary, David Powers. *Great American Brands: The Success Formulas That Made Them Famous.* New York: Fairchild Publications, 1981. 307 p.

The case history method is used for the thirty-four consumer products included in this book that includes concise marketing insights for each brand profile. An index to the marketing elements such as advertising, brand differentiation, and brand image that are discussed in each of the marketing insights and an index to product and person are provided.

507. Douglas, Gordon; Kemp, Philip; and Cook, Jeremy. *Systematic New Product Development.* 2d ed. Aldershot, Hants, England: Gower, 1978. 175 p.

The author takes a systematic approach to new product development, covering the start of a program, idea generation, brand building, research, and forecasting. The product guidelines for new products are based on experience, including cautionary concerns.

508. Ennis, F. Beaven. *Marketing Norms for Product Managers.* New York: Association of National Advertisers, 1985. 174 p.

This guidebook for the product manager presents an overview of the marketing practices necessary for developing profitable, vital products. Analyzing brand sales, interpreting market data, positioning in advertising and packaging, managing the media and promotion functions, budgeting, and developing the market plan are some areas covered.

509. Foxall, Gordon R. *Corporate Innovation: Marketing and Strategy.* New York: St. Martin's Press, 1984. 276 p.

The uncertainty accompanying the development and commercialization of new products and services for the consumer can be lessened by the role of marketing-oriented management through effective marketing-oriented innovation. Also covered are the behavior of innovative buyers and the examination of new product development as a means of reducing uncertainty.

510. Gruenwald, George. *New Product Development: What Really Works.* Chicago: Crain Books, 1985. 432 p.

Designed for those making decisions for new product programs, it traces the development of a product from need to commitment, exploration, conception, modeling, market research, and finally introduction. Case histories are used to illustrate the process.

511. *A Guide to Marketing New Industrial and Consumer Products.* Englewood Cliffs, NJ: Prentice-Hall, 1985. 106 p.

Individuals involved with the introduction of new products will find this a flexible document, usable as a checklist or timetable for the market plan. From the prototype testing through post evaluation, tasks are outlined, complete with guide pages, diagrams, graphs, and work sheets for each task section. A glossary of terms is also included.

512. Hanan, Mack. *Life-Styled Marketing: How to Position Products for Premium Profits.* rev. ed. New York: AMACOM, 1980. 159 p.

Lifestyled marketing is a systems approach to a market which includes patterns of activity, thought patterns, and self-images associated with these activities. The major attributes are psychographics, product and media usage, and demographics. Based on lifestyled marketing, this book is a guide to new opportunities for marketing existing and new products in a specific or general area. Can also be used as basis for corporate organization.

513. Hehman, Raymond D. *Product Management: Marketing in a Changing Environment.* Homewood, IL: Dow Jones-Irwin, 1984. 181 p.

This book has practical examples as well as explanations of marketing principles including sales forecasting, promotion planning, marketing research, financial planning, and use of the personal computer

514. Hoo, David. *How to Develop and Market New Products Better and Faster.* New York: Association of National Advertisers, Inc., 1985. 296 p.

Key management considerations are identified that contribute to the success of a new product. Organization and staffing are some key elements covered in this book.

515. *Management of the New Product Function: A Guidebook.* New York: Association of National Advertisers, Inc., 1980. 216 p.

Intended for the individual primarily responsible for a company's new product program, the emphasis is on the management considerations involved. The areas covered include the definition of new products, planning, organizing, staffing, directing, and the essential activities involved in new product introduction. The appendix contains reproductions of talks that cover current thinking and practices in implementing the new product process.

516. Morehead, John W. *Finding and Licensing New Products & Technology from the U.S.A.* Loose-leaf. Elk Grove Village, IL: Technology Search International.
To locate new products available for licensing, this loose-leaf binder provides names and addresses of directories and reference materials, addresses for licensing databases, exhibitions, newsletters, and other publications for new product information. More than fifty licensing, consulting, and service firms that can assist in a search are also included.

517. Palde, Kristian S. *Pricing Decisions and Marketing Policy.* Englewood Cliffs, NJ: Prentice-Hall, 1971. 116 p.
Pricing is one of the basics of marketing strategy, is especially important for a new product, and is closely related to the company's total marketing strategy. Using mathematical calculations, cost and demand factors, and pricing goals and the competitive impact on pricing, marketing mix, and product line and legal constraints on pricing are some of the areas covered.

518. Rosenau, Milton D., Jr. *Innovation: Managing the Developments of Profitable New Products.* Belmont, CA: Lifetime Learning Publications, 1982. 220 p.
New product development is a complex process and the five key factors for proper management of the innovation process are strategic issues of the company, market identification, unique product idea, profit planning, and teamwork. Illustrations, case studies, and checklists are included.

519. Schoenfeld, Gerald. *Schoenfeld's New Product Success Book.* New York: Boardroom Books, 1981. 129 p.
The techniques for developing new products are explained followed by an outline summary of these techniques. Topics include use of consumer panels, developing an idea, advertising strategies, test markets, and product launching.

520. Souder, William E. *Managing New Product Innovations.* Lexington, MA: Lexington Books, 1987. 251 p.
Based on life cycle data from 298 new product development innovations, this handbook shows the best way to manage new product innovation. Questions concerning cost and the time it takes to innovate are covered along with factors influencing project success or failure, organization decision processes, and interface between R&D and marketing.

521. Taylor, James W. *Planning Profitable New Product Strategies.* Radnor, PA: Chilton Books, 1982. 233 p.
A state-of-the-art guide that covers the steps for successfully planning new product development from initiating the thought process, generating new product concepts, developing and refining guidelines, and screening and analyzing concepts to commercialization of the product.

522. Urban, Glen L., and Hauser, John R. *Design and Marketing of New Products.* Englewood Cliffs, NJ: Prentice-Hall, 1980. 618 p.
The sequential steps for new product development covered in this book are strategy, opportunity design, testing, or implementation stages with emphasis on managerial involvement. References to additional research, a checklist for new product development, a lengthy bibliography, and an index by concept and technique are provided.

523. Weinstein, Art. *Market Segmentation: Using Demographics, Psychographics and Other Segmentation Techniques to Uncover and Exploit New Markets.* Chicago: Probus, 1987. 296 p.

A guide to segment strategies and techniques that are examined in relation to marketing and product planning. Product managers and marketing professionals can use these cost efficient means for existing products and potential new markets.

524. Wind, Yoram; Mahajan, Vijay; and Cardozo, Richard N., eds. *New-Product Forecasting: Models and Applications.* Lexington, MA: Lexington Books, 1981. 564 p.

Forecasting the success of new products is a difficult task because performance depends on a number of factors. Numerous forecasting models have been developed, but this book limits discussion to fourteen of the major new-product forecasting models, classifying them by type of data and need for implementation. An overview and utilization for each group of models is included.

525. Wizenberg, Larry, ed. *The New Products Handbook.* Homewood, IL: Dow Jones-Irwin, 1986. 337 p.

From planning through development, research, and evaluation, the techniques and strategies suggested provide for successful introduction of a new product. Marketing and new product managers, entrepreneurs, and managers of small business can benefit from this information.

PAPERS—COLLECTED

526. Rothberg, Robert R. *Corporate Strategy and Product Innovation.* 2d ed. New York: Free Press, 1981. 529 p.

A collection of classic and leading articles on a variety of new product development topics.

PERIODICALS

527. *Journal of Product Innovation Management.* Quarterly. New York: North-Holland.

Articles on theoretical structures and practical techniques are intended for the product manager involved with innovation and also for the student. The articles are based on empirical research, management observations and experience, and state-of-the art reviews of issues.

528. *Journal of Product Law.* Quarterly. Moorestown, NJ: Symposia Press.

This journal deals with the legal issues involved with the design, manufacture, and distribution of a product. Product liability is sometimes included.

529. *Journal of Products Liability.* Quarterly. Elmford, NY: Pergamon Press, Journals Division.

An international, scholarly journal publishing research on legal aspects of products, product groups, and issues in prosecution or defense of product liability. Appropriate research in technical or medical fields is also included.

530. *New Product Development.* Monthly. Point Pleasant, NJ: Research Development Marketing.

This newsletter covers trends, consumer tastes, and marketing directions with emphasis on today's thinking that shows what successful innovators want and need.

531. *New Product/New Business Digest.* Annual. Schenectady, NY: Genium Publishing Corp.
This catalog describes over 500 products and processes that are available for licensing that previously appeared in the *Venture/Product News.* Full address for the listing agency is included.

532. *Packaging.* Monthly. Boston: Cahners Publishing Co.
Developments, trends, and forecasts in the industry cover manufacturing, marketing, and R&D. Special issues are the *Annual Buyers Guide* and the *Packaging Encyclopedia & Yearbook* which can be purchased separately.

533. *Venture/Product News.* Monthly. Schenectady, NY: Genium Publishing Corp.
This illustrated newsletter lists a wide variety of available-for-license products or processes for all markets—commercial, consumer, industrial. These items are from corporatios, universities, R&D labs, government departments and agencies, and international technology clearinghouses.

TRADEMARKS/PATENTS

Guidebooks/Handbooks

534. Diamond, Sidney A. *Trademark Problems and How to Avoid Them.* rev. ed. Chicago: Crain Books, 1981. 276 p.
Using case studies, the author illustrates the many different kinds of problems that arise in the selection and protection of trademarks. These help to identify potential problems and can be avoided using proper techniques. Indexes of trademarks mentioned and cited cases are included.

535. *How to Name a New Business or a New Product.* Loose-leaf. Toronto, ON: ABC Dial, 1984. 1 vol.
In North America, more than 1,000,000 names were registered for new products and businesses in 1984. In order to avoid complications, this step-by-step guide includes case studies, examples, and trends. To check availability of a new name, see the directory of government departments in the U.S. and Canada and other reference sources.

536. Oathout, John D. *Trademarks: A Guide to the Selection, Administration and Protection of Trademarks in Modern Business Practice.* New York: Scribners, 1981. 210 p.
The basics of trademark administration, the routine, and nonlegal matters are covered in this book intended for the trademark administrator in a company; marketers, advertising agencies, and designers; and public relations people. It is not a substitute for legal counsel but identifies the times to seek legal assistance. A list of sources for trademarks and trade names is included.

537. U.S. Patent and Trademark Office. *Patent and Trademark Forms Booklet.* Washington, DC: U.S. Government Printing Office, 1979. 350 p.
These full-size, reproducible forms of frequently used patent and trademark applications are those used in filing patent and trademark cases. The law does not require the use of these or any other particular forms as long as the individual complies with the requirements set forth in the laws. The forms can be modified to fit a particular situation. Translations of twenty-three foreign languages for some of the oath and declaration forms needed in other countries are also included.

Papers—Collected

538. Spitz, Edward, ed. *Product Planning.* 2d ed. New York: Petrocelli/Charter, 1977. 412 p.

A collection of readings on product planning and management that is arranged to present a relevant flow of information. Areas covered include the systems approach, organizational approach, the planning process, product auditing, new products and the law, and trends.

PRICING

Bibliographies

539. Lund, Daulatram; Monroe, Kent; and Choudhury, Pravat K. *Pricing Policies and Strategies: An Annotated Bibliography.* Chicago: American Marketing Assn., 1982. 110 p.

A selected bibliography of journal articles and a few monographs cover topics such as cost analysis, pricing practices, pricing decisions, price administration, demand analysis, and regulation of prices. A classified arrangment is used with only an author index.

Guidebooks/Handbooks

540. Gabor, André. *Pricing: Principles and Practices.* London: Heinemann Educational Books, 1977. 276 p.

Pricing is an effective marketing tool, and fluctuation in sales can be caused by changes in absolute and relative prices. The theory of price, the difference between profit-oriented and cost-based pricing, multipricing, pricing at the retail level for services and new products, and the effect of price on consumer behavior are covered.

541. Marshall, Arthur. *More Profitable Pricing.* London: McGraw-Hill Book Co., Ltd., 1979. 109 p.

The aim of this book is to increase profits. It covers traditional pricing methods, the art and science of pricing, what the pricer needs to know, and how to install a rational pricing program.

542. Winkler, John. *Pricing for Results.* New York: Facts on File Publications, 1984. 207 p.

For many pricing situations, this book has a practical solution. Fifty-six self-assessment quizes and case histories cover topics such as price wars, instant pricing, and cost-related and market-related pricing.

ASSOCIATIONS

Packaging Institute USA. 20 Summer St., Stamford, CT 06901.

Product Development and Management Assn. c/o Thomas P. Hustad, Graduate School of Business, P.O. Box 647, Indiana University, Indianapolis, IN 46223.

U.S. Trademark Assn. Six E. 45th St., New York, NY 10017.

Personal Selling

DIRECTORIES

543. *Directory of Conventions.* Annual. Philadelphia, PA: Bill Communications, Inc.

More than 23,000 listings of meetings and conventions held by U.S. and Canadian organizations are arranged chronologically within geographic areas. These are also indexed by eighty-two different industries and professions. Included are the dates; whether regional or statewide, national or international meetings; place for the meeting; commercial exhibits planned; projected total attendance; and name of executive in charge. Kept up to date by midyear supplements.

544. *Directory of Firms Marketing through Manufacturers Representatives.* Annual. New York: MacRae's Blue Book, Inc.

More than 15,000 manufacturer's representatives are listed in this directory which is organized geographically and by product.

545. Elster, Robert J., ed. *Trade Shows and Professional Exhibits.* 2d ed. Detroit, MI: Gale Research Co., 1987. 915 p.

This directory focuses on the shows with the greatest attendance and greatest number of exhibitors. Detailed information on conferences, conventions, trade and industrial shows, expositions, merchandise marts, and expositions includes attendance figures, cost and number of exhibits, dates and locations for five years, and much more. Geographic, chonological, subject, organization, and name/keyword indexes are provided. Kept up to date by *Trade Shows and Professional Exhibits Directory: Supplement* with detailed entries for additional exhibit opportunities.

546. *Exhibits Schedule: Annual Directory of Trade and Industrial Shows.* Annual. New York: Bill Communications, Inc.

A list of over 6,000 show sponsors holding more than 11,000 trade shows and exhibits in the U.S. and throughout the world. The entries are listed by industry, location, and date. Included are the name of the event and sponsoring organization, frequency, number of booths and square feet planned, projected total attendance, name of hotel/convention center, and the name of the executive in charge. July supplements update the annual listing.

547. *Nationwide Directory of Major Mass Market Merchandisers.* Annual. New York: Salesman's Guide, Inc.

A directory, except for New York City, of men's, women's, and children's apparel and accessory buyers for 2,000 of the leading discount stores, variety, supermarket, and drug chains.

GUIDEBOOKS/HANDBOOKS

548. Birnes, William, and Markman, Gary. *Selling at the Top: The 100 Best Companies to Sell for in America Today.* New York: Harper & Row, 1985. 338 p.

The five best companies in various areas of the service, consumer goods, and light and heavy industries are ranked by compensation, commission, support, and intangibles for salespeople.

549. Delmar, Ken. *Winning Moves: The Body Language of Selling.* New York: Warner Books, 1984. 299 p.

This book assists the salesperson with a practical blend of applied observation, behavioral psychology, and acting techniques to interpret and use nonverbal signals to sell more effectively.

550. Enzer, Michael J. *Selling by Seminar.* Homewood, IL: Dow Jones-Irwin, 1986. 150 p,

Selling by seminar is another technique to increase sales by providing a selected group of interested people information about a product or service without making a sales presentation. The step-by-step procedure to implement the method and examples of documents needed for the seminar such as invitations, seating plans, and feedback questionnaires are included in this book.

551. Good, Bill. *Prospecting Your Way to Sales Success: How to Find New Business by Phone.* New York: Scribners/Macmillan, 1986. 242 p.

A guide to designing a complete, customized telephone prospecting campaign that explains how to qualify prospective customers, how to design an appropriate sales message, how to develop and test scripts for a variety of products, and how and when to close.

552. Grikscheit, Gary M.; Cash, Harold C.; and Crissy, W. J. T. *Handbook of Selling: Psychological, Managerial and Marketing Bases.* New York: Wiley, 1981. 671 p.

For sales people and students of selling, basic objectives and concepts that promote effective selling are covered. Explanations of communication, the importance of understanding the buyer's characteristics, group selling, and the techniques for using the visual and auditory learning channel to maximize sales effectiveness are included.

553. Hanlon, Al. *Creative Selling through Trade Shows.* New York: Hawthorn Books, Inc., 1977. 244 p.

The guidelines in this book cover the proven techniques and advantages of trade shows. Areas covered include costs, selecting an exhibit house, setting objectives, exhibit design, booking sales at the show, hospitality suites, and evaluating the investment.

554. Konikow, Robert B. *How to Participate Profitably in Trade Shows: Including Step-by-Step Methods to Design, Build and Staff Business Producing Exhibits at Low Cost.* rev. ed. Loose-leaf. Chicago: Dartnell Corp., 1985.

This loose-leaf publication includes techniques for determining objectives; designing, building, and staffing exhibit's at low cost; and determining the exhibit's effectiveness. Checklists and a planning guide facilitate the development of this type of sales promotion.

555. Krause, William H. *How to Get Started as a Manufacturer's Representative.* New York: AMACOM, 1980. 207 p.

Intended for the person who wants his own sales agency but doesn't know how to begin, the author provides information on what an independent manufacturer's representative does, how to find good products to sell, setting up an agency and the key to survival.

556. Massimino, Sal T. *The Complete Book of Closing Sales.* New York: AMACOM, 1981. 154 p.

Without the closing of a sale, no other steps have meaning. This book covers areas such as listening to prospects, ways to hold the buyer's attention, give-to-get selling, nonstop selling, and follow-up selling techniques, including 250 successful closing lines. Information for the sales manager as trainer and motivator is also provided.

557. Miller, Robert B., and Heiman, Stephen. *Strategic Selling: The Unique Sales System Proven Successful by America's Best Companies.* New York: William Morrow, 1985. 319 p.

This book covers the "Win-Win" approach to selling which is concerned with the customer's needs. The basic elements of strategic selling are covered along with the multiaccount strategies of managing your time, focusing on the customer, and developing an action plan.

558. Rogers, Robert S., and Chamberlain, V. B. *National Account Marketing Handbook.* New York: AMACOM, 1981. 292 p.

All aspects of national account marketing are covered from definitions, identification of the characteristics of the national account, legal and international aspects, and selling to the federal government.

559. Shook, Robert L. *The Perfect Sales Presentation.* New York: Bantam Books, 1986. 293 p.

The selling techniques presented in this book are based on actual experiences that have been field tested by five sales experts. The areas covered include doing your homework before the presentation, getting past the gatekeeper at the telephone, creating interest in the product, fact finding about the prospect, the actual presentation, overcoming objections, closing the sale, and service to the customer.

PERIODICALS

560. *Agency Sales Magazine.* Monthly. Irvine, CA: Manufacturer's Agents National Assn.

This periodical covers items of interest to independent sales representatives, their suppliers and customers, and the manufacturers who sell through sales persons.

561. *The American Salesman: The National Magazine for Sales Professionals.* Monthly. Burlington, IA: National Research Bureau, Inc.

The articles cover a range of topics and give practical advice for the salesperson whether a beginner or an experienced individual. Many are motivational in nature.

562. *The National Voice of Salesmen.* Quarterly. New York: National Council of Salesmen's Organizations.

Items of interest for sales representatives from all industries also includes information about legislation affecting commissioned salespeople.

563. *Opportunity.* Monthly. Chicago: Opportunity Press, Inc.

Practical articles aimed at the salesperson cover methods, management, career evaluation, and products and include profiles of successful salespeople.

564. *Personal Selling Power.* 8/yr. Fredericksburg, VA: Gerhard Gschwandtner & Associates.

For those involved in selling, this newspaper-type publication has articles on selling skills and techniques, motivation, sales management, and new technologies. Reports on surveys of various topics that were conducted by the publisher are included.

565. *Salesmanship.* Bimonthly. Chicago: Dartnell Corp.

A newsletter that concentrates on practical selling ideas with how-to orientation from opening and closing a sales, winning customer confidence, to writing effective sales letters. Self-evaluation features also assist in training salespeople.

566. *Successful Woman.* Monthly. Sacramento, CA: National Association for Professional Saleswomen.

Items of interest and information for women actively involved in sales.

PROCEEDINGS

567. Jacoby, Jacob, and Craig, C. Samuel. *Personal Selling: Theory, Research and Practice.* Lexington, MA: Lexington Books, 1984. 316 p.

These scholarly conference papers cover topics such as principles of automatic influence, bargaining behavior in personal selling, improving effectiveness of a salesperson's time, sales effectiveness, job performance, and issues in retail selling. Sponsored by the Association for Consumer Research.

ASSOCIATIONS

Incentive Manufacturers Representatives Association. 110 Pennsylvania Ave., Oreland, PA 19075.

International Exhibitors Association. 5103-B Backlick Rd., Annandale, VA 22003.

National Account Marketing Association. 50 E. 41st St., New York, NY 10017.

National Association of Professional Saleswomen. P.O. Box 255708, Sacramento, CA 95865.

National Association of Sales and Marketing Professionals. 1130 Berkshire Lane, Newport Beach, CA 92660.

National Council of Salesmen's Organizations. 225 Broadway, Room 515, New York, NY 10007.

Professional Salespersons of America. P.O. Box 10285, 100 Maria Circle, N.W., Albuquerque, NM 87184.

Women in Sales Association. Eight Madison Ave., Valhalla, NY 10595.

Physical Distribution/Logistics

ABSTRACTS

568. *Marketing & Distribution Abstracts.* 8/yr. Wembley, England: Institute of Marketing, Anbar Publications, Ltd.

Published in association with the Institute of Marketing in England, this current awareness service lists recent articles in British and American journals, alphabetically by the title of the journal, not by the subject. This publication is intended for a quick overview of recently published articles.

BIBLIOGRAPHIES

569. Davis, Bob J. *Information Sources in Transportation, Material Management and Physical Distribution.* Westport, CT: Greenwood Press, 1976. 715 p.

This annotated bibliography has more than 10,000 citations to books, directories, guides, government publications, and periodicals, trade and professional organizations. The citations are divided into more than sixty transportation subject categories.

570. LaLonde, Bernard J. *Supplement to Bibliography on Logistics and Physical Distribution Management.* Annual. Oak Brook, IL: Council of Logistics Management.

This annual supplement updates the *Bibliography on Physical Distribution Management* originally published in 1967. References are to material published during the previous calendar year including books, journals, newsletters, and trade publications covering areas such as logistics concepts, legal sources, statistical techniques, cost analysis, regulatory reform, materials management, and logistics planning.

571. Lund, Daulatram, et al. *Marketing Distribution: A Selected and Annotated Bibliography.* Chicago: American Marketing Assn., 1979. 118 p.

The view of channels of distribution is from the total systems concept also including the underlying principles of marketing science. The three areas covered are exchange systems, social systems, and logistics systems. The articles, selected from forty-two journals, were published primarily from 1960 to 1979.

DICTIONARIES

572. Cavinato, Joseph L. *Transportation-Logistics Dictionary*. Washington, DC: Traffic Service Corp., 1982. 323 p.
Definitions and explanations reflect the changes in transportation regulations, developments in the industry, cost impacts, and productivity concerns.

DIRECTORIES

573. *Official Directory of Industrial and Commercial Traffic Executives*. Annual. Washington, DC: Traffic Service Corp.
More than 26,000 executives managing traffic and transportation in industrial and commercial firms are listed. Section one is a list of organizations, bureaus, and other agencies important to traffic executives. Section two is an alphabetical listing of companies. Secton three is an alphabetical list of executives.

GUIDEBOOKS/HANDBOOKS

574. Blanding, Warren. *Practical Handbook of Distribution/Customer Service*. Washington, DC: Traffic Service Corp., 1985. 564 p.
The emphasis of this book is on practical plans and the results that can be viewed on the bottom line. Little theory is included, but principles, procedures, and case histories illustrate how customer service is important to the company. The information can be used in an existing department as well as for planning and organizing a customer service department. Tables, forms, questionnaires, graphs, and charts are included.

575. Christopher, Martin. *The Strategy of Distribution Management*. Westport, CT: Quorum Books, 1985. 182 p.
Logistics is the management of the flow of products from the sources of supply to the point of consumption. This flow involves the business with customer service and marketing, costs, information systems, distribution planning, and supply channel strategy. The managerial issues involved in the development and implementation of the distribution strategy are covered in this book.

576. Frey, Stephen L. *Management's Guide to Efficient Money-Saving Warehousing*. Chicago: Dartnell Corp., 1982. 363 p.
A step-by-step guide to practices of cost-efficient warehousing for supervisors and executives, this is a collection of accepted operating procedures for receiving, storage, stock selection, shipping, regulations on hazardous materials, energy conservation, and equipment selection.

577. Heyel, Carl, ed. *The VNR Concise Guide to Business Logistics*. New York: Van Nostrand, 1979. 134 p.
Basic information on transportation, warehousing, materials handling, supply scheduling, and related activities are covered for the executive who is involved in other areas of management.

578. Magee, John F.; Copacino, William C.; and Rosenfield, Donald B. *Modern Logistics Management: Integrating Marketing, Manufacturing and Physical Distribution*. New York: Wiley, 1985. 430 p.
This book covers the concept of a logistic system including the elements forming the system, the development of systems analysis and network design, the issues of long-term planning, and the organization and management of the logistics function.

579. Patton, Joseph D. *Logistics Technology and Management: The New Approach: A Comprehensive Handbook for Commerce, Industry and Government.* New York: Solomon Press, 1986. 338 p.

> A comprehensive overview of logistics management that provides proven methods and models that help a business or organization increase profits and use of resources. A bibliography of sources is included.

580. Robeson, James F., and House, Robert G. *The Distribution Handbook.* New York: Free Press, 1985. 970 p.

> Those interested in distribution will find this reference book has practical, how-to information on a wide variety of topics. The material applies to all levels of distribution—producer, wholesaler, and retailer—with emphasis on the total-channel or producer's perspective.

PERIODICALS

581. *Chilton's Distribution for Traffic and Transportation Decision Makers.* Monthly. Radnor, PA: Chilton Co.

> A trade journal for the manager in charge of physical distribution covering current developments in distribution and management for all types of freight and traffic management. The *International Guide* in the July issue is a directory of trucking lines, ports, ocean carriers, transportation and distribution equipment, and public warehouses.

582. *Handling and Shipping Management: The Physical Distribution Magazine.* Monthly. Cleveland, OH: Penton/PC.

> For the manager of distribution, logistics, traffic, and transportation, this magazine provides news on physical distribution and happenings of interest to the industry, legal briefs, management of personnel, products, use of computers, and status and business activity of public companies in the transportation industry.

583. *International Journal of Physical Distribution and Materials Management.* 8/yr. Bradford, West Yorkshire, England: MCB Publications.

> Scholarly papers present research on problems and techniques in physical distribution and management. Usually every other issue is devoted to a specific topic in the field.

584. *Journal of Business Logistics.* Semiannual. Oak Brook, IL: National Council of Physical Distribution Management.

> A blend of theoretical and practical material covering new information on logistics operations and management, emerging theory and techniques, and researched thought and practice in related areas of logistics management.

585. *Journal of Purchasing and Materials Management.* Quarterly. Oradell, NJ: National Association of Purchasing Management.

> Scholarly articles discuss theory, principles, and application; report research; and evaluate techniques and concepts from business, economics, information systems, and the behavioral sciences in areas of purchasing and materials management.

586. *The Logistics and Transportation Review.* Quarterly. Vancouver, BC: Faculty of Commerce and Business Administraion, University of British Columbia.

> A scholarly, international journal for research papers on logistics and transportation that emphasize the quantitative approach.

587. *Traffic Management.* Monthly. Denver, CO: Cahners Publishing Co.
All types of transportation, warehousing, and distribution involved in the handling and movement of goods are covered in this publication. The *Transportation/Distribution Directory* in the March issue lists sources for services, product location, and a list of transportation/distribution publications.

588. *Traffic World.* Weekly. Washington, DC: Traffic Service Corp.
This weekly news magazine covers recent developments in transportation, federal regulatory news, and federal and state legislation.

PROCEEDINGS

589. Council of Logistics Management. *Annual Conference Proceedings.* Annual. Oak Brook, IL: The Council.
The papers included in this conference series cover a variety of topics related to the logistics of management, career information, compensation trends, and a list of related software packages.

590. Harvey, Michael G., and Lusch, Robert F. *Marketing Channels: Domestic and International Perspectives.* Chicago: American Marketing Assn., 1982. 171 p.
Papers presented at this workshop covered marketing channel theory and practice with specific topics such as physical distribution and logistics, channel strategy, structure, and management.

ASSOCIATIONS

American Society of Transportation and Logistics. P.O. Box 33095, Louisville, KY 40232.

Association of Transportation Practitioners. 1211 Connecticut Ave., N.W., Suite 310, Washington, DC 20036.

Council of Logistics Management. 2803 Butterfield Rd., Suite 380, Oak Brook, IL 60521.

International Material Management Society. 650 E. Higgins Rd., Schaumburg, IL 60195.

National Institute of Packaging, Handling, and Logistic Engineers. P.O. Box 2765, Arlington, VA 22202.

Retailing

DATABASES

591. D&B-Dun's Electronic Yellow Pages–Retailers Directory. Current coverage. Mountain Lakes, NJ: Dun's Marketing Services. (Vendor: DIAL)

The database has information from yellow page directories throughout the U.S. covering a range of retail establishments. In addition to name, address, and telephone number, the county name, modified four-digit SIC code, assets, and estimate of city population are included.

592. D&B-Dun's Electronic Yellow Pages–Wholesalers Directory. Current coverage. Westport, CT: Market Data Retrieval, Inc. (Vendor: DIAL)

Database listings are from more than 4,800 telephone directories throughout the U.S. covering a wide range of wholesalers. Records include name, address, telephone number, county, SIC code, size of the city, and type of listing.

DICTIONARIES

593. Knight, John B., and Salter, Charles A., eds. *Knight's Foodservice Dictionary*. New York: CBI Book/Van Nostrand, 1987. 393 p.

Definitions from all aspects of the food service industry cover areas such as basic ingredients, cost control, culinary arts, equipment, management information systems, sanitation, safety, service, and merchandising. Continual updating is planned to reflect new trends and ideas.

594. Kreiger, Murray. *The Complete Dictionary of Buying and Merchandising: 1127 Words, Terms, Expressions and Abbreviations Commonly Used in Buying and Merchandising*. New York: National Retail Merchants Assn., 1980. 124 p.

These specialized terms are briefly defined, and an addendum of over 180 words is also provided.

595. Ostrow, Rona, and Smith, Sweetman R. *The Dictionary of Retailing*. New York: Fairchild Publications, 1985. 256 p.

Terms and phrases for stores, shopping centers, merchandising, data processing, accounting, personnel management in retailing, direct marketing, marketing resarch, mail order, and consumer behavior are defined in this nontechnical dictionary. Retail associations and capsule biographies of historical figures associated with retail marketing are also included.

DIRECTORIES

596. *The Chain Store Guide Market Directories.* Annual. New York: CSG Information Services, Lebhar-Friedman. 19 vols.

These directories provide basic information found in most directories and also includes financial profiles covering sales figures, number of stores, sales per square foot, and date of founding. Information is arranged geographically by states. Available as a set or as individual volumes. The titles of the directories are:

Auto Aftermarket Suppliers.
CE, Photography and Major Appliance Retailers and Distributors.
Chain Restaurant Operators.
Computers + Software Retailers.
Cooperatives, Voluntaries & Wholesale Grocers.
Country Clubs.
Department Stores/Mail Order Firms.
Discount Department Stores/Catalog Showrooms.
Drug & HBA Chains/Drug Wholesalers.
Food Service Distributors.
General Merchandise/Variety & Specialty Stores.
Hardlines Distributors.
High-Volume Independent Restaurants.
Home Center Operators & Hardware Chains.
Home Furnishing Retailers.
Men's & Boy's Wear Specialty Stores.
Supermarket, Grocery & Convenience Store Chains.
Value Added Resellers.
Women's & Children's Wear Specialty Stores.

597. *Directory of Shopping Centers in the United States and Canada.* Annual. Chicago: National Research Bureau, Inc.

Published in four regional volumes—Eastern, Midwestern, Southern, and the West—the entries are geographically arranged. Information includes the name of the center developer, manager, size, sales, cost of the centers, and the names of the tenants. A fact sheet for each state is at the beginning of the section. Various indexes such as major owners, gross leaseable area, and new or planned centers are included.

598. *Phelon's Discount Stores.* Annual. Fairview, NJ: Phelon, Sheldon & Marsar, Inc.

This directory of more than 4,000 self-service, discount stores, catalog showrooms, drug chains, and lease operations also includes *Sheldon's Jobbing & Wholesale Directory*. The businesses are listed geographically and include the names of owners, officers, and buyers. Another section lists more than 400 companies that buy and resell merchandise to retailers, wholesale distributors to retailers, and maintain racks of merchandise in drug stores and supermarkets.

599. *Phelon's Women's Apparel Shops.* Biannual. New York: Phelon, Shelden & Marsar, Inc.

More than 15,000 women's specialty shops are listed giving the number of branches, square feet per store, buyers, merchandise managers, store's estimate of its quality and price range. Does not overlap with *Sheldon's Retail Directory.*

600. *Progressive Grocers Marketing Guidebook: The Book of Supermarket Distributions.* Annual. Stamford, CT: Progressive Grocer Information Sales.

This directory divides retail and wholesale grocery companies into seven regions and gives statistics about the industry as a whole and regional data. Information about market areas in each state includes company buying data and personnel.

601. *Sheldon's Retail Directory of the United States and Canada and Phelon's Resident Buyers and Merchandise Brokers.* Annual. New York: Phelon, Sheldon & Marsar, Inc.
   This directory lists department stores; chains and independent companies; women's, men's, and children's specialty stores; and variety and furniture stores. Entries are arranged geographically including the name and locations of stores, department buyers, merchandise and advertising managers, and purchasing agents. Another section lists resident buyers and merchandise brokers arranged alphabetically, including the lines of merchandise bought.

602. *Thomas Grocery Register.* Annual. New York: Thomas Publishing Co. 3 vols.
   Manufacturers and processors of food, equipment supplies, machinery, importers, and services are included. Volume one lists sales and distribution including the names of supermarket chains, convenience stores, institutional buyers, wholesalers, manufacturers, agents, and other. Volume two is arranged by product and services, alphabetically by state and city. Volume three is a listing by company with an index of brand names. The "Food Marketers Handbook" is included in the set.

GUIDEBOOKS/HANDBOOKS

603. Allen, Randy L. *Bottom Line Issues in Retailing: The Touche Ross Guide to Retail Management.* Radnor, PA: Chilton Book Co., 1984. 294 p.
   Some issues facing retailers are merchandise management, information processing, retail accounting, business planning, and store operations. The approach to these issues is quantitative. Identifying needed data, means of gathering data, converting this information into action to increase productivity, and profitability are some areas covered.

604. Guberman, Reuben. *Handbook of Retail Promotion Ideas.* Reading, MA: Addison-Wesley, 1981. 258 p.
   The function of promotions is to attract customers to spend money and to impress the name of the business on the public. The promotion suggestions in this book cover a wide range of possibilities adaptable to a particular business. Some activities suggested include children's art contests, team sponsorship, and radio remotes. Each item is analyzed by whom it reaches, what it does, and the costs. Sample press releases and a promotion organizer worksheet are included.

605. Howe, Judith J. *Training for Retail Sales and Profit.* New York: AMACOM, 1981. 237 p.
   Employee payrolls account for almost 50 percent of the operating expenses of a business. To ensure profitability, the development of a trained sales force includes not only orientation training, staff development, and improving sales performance, but also evaluating the results in view of the costs of the program. These and other topics are covered in this guide.

606. Kane, Bernard. *Retail Development Planning: A Comprehensive Guide to Successful Growth.* New York: Fairchild Publications. 1982. 125 p.
   For those responsible for the physical aspects of retail business growth, this book provides a guide to comprehensive planning. Precise instructions explain how to proceed from determining the present financial and physical structure and the future direction of the business to doing field studies, assembling prototype store plans, investigating leases, and developing the final plan, including the capital budget.

607. Lemmon, Wayne A. *The Owner's and Manager's Market Analysis Workbook for Small to Moderate Retail and Service Establishments.* New York: AMACOM, 1980. 230 p.

Using the techniques outlined in this book, the small to moderate retail or service establishment owner can do basic market analysis to determine the profitability of locating a business in a specific market location.

608. Ocko, Judy Young, and Rosenblum, M. L. *Advertising Handbook for Retail Merchants: You're the Secret Ingredient in Good Ads.* New York: National Retail Merchants Assn., 1981. 126 p.

Practical advice on how to use advertising to the best advantage whether it is catalogs, mail inserts, radio, or television, also covers measuring results, judging copy, graphics, working with agencies, media staffs, and consultants.

609. Raphel, Murray. *The Complete Food Marketing Handbook.* Washington, DC: Food Marketing Institute, 1983. 94 p.

Using ads that worked, successful ideas for food marketing from headline writing to selling specific merchandise are shown. Print advertising, sales coupons, direct mail, promotions for holidays, and image building are covered.

610. Thompson, John S. *Site Selection.* New York: Lebhar-Friedman Books, 1982. 220 p.

A practical guide organized to quickly retrieve specific information needed by those involved in retail site location analysis or shopping center development.

PAPERS—COLLECTED

611. Davies, R. L., and Rogers, D. S., eds. *Store Location and Store Assessment Research.* New York: Wiley, 1984. 375 p.

A collection of essays that discuss store location research and store assessment for the United States and the United Kingdom. They cover the retail setting, statistical information for market and site appraisals, methods and techniques for store location, sales forecasting, and evaluating retail performance.

PERIODICALS

612. *Chain Store Age General Merchandise Edition.* Monthly. New York: Lebhar-Friedman, Inc.

The chain stores covered in this trade journal include general merchandise discount, department, variety, catalog apparel, and specialty stores. Articles report on management operations, finance, trends, merchandise lines, and new products. An annual article on the state of the industry analyzes the financial performance of leading retail chains ranking the stores by volume of sales.

613. *Dealerscope Merchandising: The Marketing Magazine for Consumer Electronics and Major Appliance Retailing.* Monthly. Philadelphia, PA: North American Publishing Co.

A trade publication covering news, trends, new products, techniques for improving sales, marketing tips, industry information, and an annual directory of distributors and manufacturers' representatives is provided.

614. *Discount Merchandiser.* Monthly. New York: Schwartz Publications.
A trade journal for stores selling at low margins, covers topics such as management, sales, space allocations, and shopping habits of discount shoppers. Annual articles in May and June are statistical features that are a two-part survey of marketing data and profiles of leading discount chain stores.

615. *Discount Store News.* Biweekly. New York: Lebhar-Friedman, Inc.
Financial and marketing developments, profitability, consumer, and economic trends are covered for the full-line and specialty discount department store industry. Data are based on industry sources, research firms, and the research of the journal staff.

616. *Drug Store News.* Biweekly. New York: Lebhar-Friedman, Inc.
For the wholesale and retail drug industry, this trade journal covers operations and finance, distribution, regulations, sales, and merchandising. Annual statistical features include marketing data, advertising expenditures, marketing operations, and financial performances.

617. *Independent Restaurants.* Monthly. Madison, WI: EIP, Inc.
A trade magazine covering topics such as the marketing of restaurant service, how-others-are-doing-it, personnel, menu ideas, product review, and restauranteur of distinction.

618. *Journal of Retailing.* Quarterly. New York: Institute of Retail Management, New York University.
Some areas covered in this scholarly journal include buyer behavior, organization behavioral theory, and computers. The "Executive Summary" section provides the retailer with a practical, concise report of the theoretical articles that interest academicians.

619. *Merchandising.* Monthly. New York: Gralla Publications.
Aimed at the retailer of home electronics, major appliances, and housewares, this trade journal reports development and trends in the market. Two special features are annual statistical tables covering sales and an annual national consumer attitude survey.

620. *NRA News.* Monthly. Washington DC: National Restaurant Assn.
Food service industry trends and developments covering areas such as sales, employment, food prices, government regulations. Annual features cover statistical data on trends and forecasts.

621. *Progressive Grocer: The Magazine of Supermarketing.* Monthly. Stamford, CT: Progressive Grocer Co.
A trade magazine covering topics such as remodeling, marketing mix of products, use of computers, and personnel. Several special reports are included: "Supermarket Sales Manual" examines product performance of food and nonfood products; the "Nielsen Review of Retail Grocery Trends"; and the statistical "Annual Report of the Grocery Industry."

622. *Retail Control.* Bimonthly. New York: National Retail Merchants Assn., Financial Executives Division.
Aimed at the financial executive, the articles are on various topics such as consumer trends, data processing, inventory managment, financial management, internal audits, and taxation.

623. *Stores: The Magazine for the Retail Executive.* Monthly. New York: National Retail Merchants Assn.

A trade journal covering information on a variety of retail stores and products. Special features are listings of the 100 top specialty chains, top retail ads, top radio and TV ads, and best store displays.

624. *Supermarket Business.* Monthly. New York: Fieldmark Media, Inc.

Articles and news reports cover products, equipment, services, technology, store design, relevant legislative developments. An annual "Consumer Expenditure Study" details sales by department, spending, state and U.S. statistics on store sales, and rankings.

PROCEEDINGS

625. Brief, Arthur P., ed. *Managing Human Resources in Retail Organizations.* Lexington, MA: Lexington Books, 1984. 169 p.

The papers in this book were presented at a conference sponsored by the Institute of Retail Management and Korn/Ferry International, Inc. They cover goal setting as a means of boosting employee morale, a review of the literature on appraisal review, stress management, and techniques for improving employee productivity.

626. Pellegrini, Luca, and Reddy, Srinivask. *Marketing Channels: Relationship and Performance.* Lexington, MA: Lexington Books, 1986. 209 p.

These papers, presented at the Third International Conference on Distribution represent the current state of research on the intersection of retail management and economics. The broad categories covered include vertical agreements, issues in channel coordination, and location strategy and forecasting demand.

STATISTICAL INFORMATION

627. *Beverage Marketing Report System.* Annual. New York: Beverage Marketing.

Information on the beverage industry covers current, historical, and projected market data in separate reports. The data include consumption, market segment, distribution channels, advertising expenditures, leading brands, industry pricing, demographics of consumers, and market projections. The titles of the reports are:
Beverage Consumer.
Beverage Packaging.
Imported Beer Market & Packaging Report.
U.S. Beer Market and Packaging Report.
U.S. Bottled Water Market and Packaging Report.
U.S. Fruit Beverage Market and Packaging Report.
U.S. Soft Drink Market and Packaging Report.
U.S. Wine Market and Packaging Report.

628. *Drug Store Market Guide: A Detailed Distribution Analysis.* Annual. Mohegan Lake, NY: Drug Store Market Guide.

Regional editions of this directory provide demographic information, sales projections for every county, share-of-the-market estimates, product lines of brokers and rack jobbers, and wholesalers in the area. The stores are arranged geographically and include sales analysis, executive personnel, and buyers' names.

629. *Fairchild Fact Files.* Annual. New York: Fairchild Publications.

These market research reports contain the latest available statistical and analytical data from various sources. Coverage includes value of shipments, industry concentration, materials consumer, imports/exports, retail sales, advertising, consumer buying habits. The focus is on fashion and hard goods, and they are useful for forecasting production, promotion, and financial policies. The titles are:

Department Store Sales.
Dresses (Women's, Misses' and Juniors').
Fashion Accessories (Men and Women).
Footwear (Men, Women, Boys and Girls).
Home Textiles.
Hosiery/Legwear (Men, Women and Children).
Household Furniture and Bedding. Biannually.
Infants', Toddlers', Girls', and Boys' Wear.
Major Appliances and Electric Housewares.
Men's Furnishings and Work Wear.
Men's Sportswear, Casual Wear, Jeans.
Men's Tailored Clothing/Separate and Rainwear.
Sports/Fitness/Leisure Markets.
Sportswear, Casual Wear, Separate, Jeans (Women's, Misses' & Juniors').
A Statistical Analysis of Retailing.
Tabletop & Giftware.
The Textile/Apparel Industries: Industry Overview.
Toiletries, Cosmetics, Fragrances, and Beauty Aids.
Women's Coats, Suits, Rainwear and Furs.
Women's Inner Fashions: Nightwear, Daywear and Loungewear.

630. *Fairchild's Financial Manual of Retail Stores.* Annual. New York: Fairchild Publications.

Corporate profiles of more than 400 of the largest publicly held stores include officers and business activities, names and addresses of divisions, sales and earnings, assets and liabilities, stock information, and statistical summaries. Included are the leading food, drug, and shoe chains; department and specialty stores; mass merchandisers; discounters; and retailers.

631. *Financial Operating Results of Department and Specialty Stores.* Annual. New York: National Retail Merchants Assn.

Based on survey responses, this report includes information on financial and operating trends, retail credit operating results, sales, trends by census division, selected states and cities, performance guidelines, sales by geographic division, and operating results.

632. *Food Marketing Industry Speaks.* Annual. Washington, DC: Food Marketing Institute. 2 vols.

Volume one is a narrative summary report covering trend data on U.S. economic conditions, financial performance, and operation. Volume two has detailed tabulations of data for wholesale and retail operations.

633. German, Gene A., and Hawkes, Gerard F. *Operating Results of Self-Service Discount Department Stores and the Mass Retailers' Merchandising Report.* Biannual. New York: National Mass Retailing Institute.

Reports for these retailers are combined to provide financial and operational data for a five-year period. Useful for comparison, company analysis, and retail trends.

634. *Harris Bank Annual Retail Study.* Annual. Chicago: Harris Trust and Savings Bank.

An analysis of industry trends that covers a selected number of department stores, mass merchandisers, and specialty stores. Separate aggregate financial data and analytical observations are given for closely held retailers. Balance sheet data are supplied for publicly held companies.

635. May, Eleanor, G.; Ress, C. William; and Salmon, Walter J. *Future Trends in Retailing: Merchandise Line Trends and Store Trends 1980-1990.* Cambridge, MA: Marketing Science Institute, 1985.

The prediction that growth in retail sales is projected to be 2.3 percent per year during this decade is based on demographic factors, psychographics, customer lifestyles, internal effect, merchandise line changes, and institutional-type changes. Also covered are the economy and store trends.

636. *National Total-Market Audit.* Annual. New York: Audits & Surveys, Co., Inc.

For those marketing consumer products, this report provides information on retail sales, retailer inventories, retailer purchases, product availability of their brands and competitive brands. These data are for many product categories and for all major types of outlets.

637. *Progressive Grocer's Market Scope.* Annual. New York: Progressive Grocer Publishing Co.

This annual includes statistical information and share of the market by chains, supermarkets, and wholesalers. The title varies and is sometimes cited *Market Scope.*

638. *Retailing for the 1980's: A Strategic and Financial Analysis.* New York: Dun & Bradstreet, Inc., 1983. 125 p.

An analysis of the retail industry, with emphasis on thirteen segments that are analyzed in terms of sales, profits, new businesses, failures, industry norms, and rations. The key issues affecting retailing in the 1980s are also covered.

639. *Trends: Consumer Attitudes and the Supermarket.* Annual. Washington, DC: Food Marketing Institute, Research Department.

A survey of consumers that covers economic concerns, supermarket industry practices and performances, and shopping patterns. Comparative data from previous surveys in the 80s is included.

640. U.S. Bureau of the Census. *Current Retail Trade Reports.* Washington, DC: U.S. Government Printing Office.

This is a series of five publications covering various time spans that reports comparative data, estimates of sales, inventories, and other measures depending on the type of report. The series titles are:
Advance Monthly Retail Sales.
Annual Retail Trade Report.
Monthly Retail Sales.
Monthly Retail Trade Report.
Weekly Retail Sales Report.

641. U.S. Bureau of the Census. *1982 Census of Retail Trade.* Every 5 years. Washington, DC: U.S. Government Printing Office.

Includes establishments that sell merchandise for personal or household consumption. Coverage is of the U.S., states, SCSA, SMSA, county, minicipalities of 2,500 inhabitants or more and major retail centers. Data are arranged by SIC numbers covering the numbers of establishments, sales, ranking by sales, and payrolls. These census are updated every five years.

ASSOCIATIONS

American Retail Federation. 1616 H St., N.W., Washington, DC 20006.

Association of General Merchandise Chains. 1625 Eye St., N.W., Washington, DC 20006.

Association of Retail Marketing Services. 412 Ocean Ave., Sea Bright, NJ 07760.

Food Marketing Institute. 1750 K St., N.W., Washington, DC 20006.

National Association of Retail Dealers of America. 2 N. Riverside Plaza, Chicago, IL 60606.

National Mass Retailing Institute. 570 Seventh Ave., New York, NY 10018.

National Retail Merchants Assn. 100 W. 31st St., New York, NY 10001.

Purdue University Retail Institute. 101 Young Graduate House, West Lafayette, IN 47907.

Sales Management

BIBLIOGRAPHIES

642. Bellenger, Danny N.; Berl, Robert L.; and Traylor, M. Denise. *Sales Management: A Review of the Current Literature.* Atlanta, GA: College of Business Administration, Georgia State University, 1981. 90 p.

The articles are from selected academic journals published in the 1970s. The abstracts for eighty-eight selected articles summarize the findings and methodology. The topical arrangement includes headings such as communication, ethics and law, evaluation and supervision, forecasting, quotas. A bibliography of an additional 251 articles is arranged alphabetically by the author's name.

643. Chonko, Lawrence B., and Enis, Ben M., eds. *Selling and Sales Management: A Bibliography.* Chicago: American Marketing Assn., 1980. 74 p.

Using the Personal Selling Model, the articles are organized by this plan and include more than 300 annotated citations for categories such as boundary relations, economic process, exchange, and organization.

GUIDEBOOKS/HANDBOOKS

644. Anderson, George B. *How to Make Your Sales' Meetings Come Alive.* Chicago: Dartnell Corp., 1976. 350 p.

This manual provides practical information on how to plan sales meetings that get and hold attention, shake up complacency, set the competitive pace, and provide ways to introduce a new sales campaign.

645. Barry, John W., and Henry, Porter. *Effective Sales Incentive Compensation.* New York: McGraw-Hill, 1981. 213 p.

This book discusses the rationale of sales incentive plans, objectives, and methods of evaluating an existing plan. Sales compensation is regarded as a marketing tool and should interest marketing executives. Compensation plans are included for field sales executives, wholesalers, and retailers. Because each company has different needs, no model plans are included.

646. Birsner, E. Patricia, and Balsley, Ronald D. *Practical Guide to Customer Service Management and Operations.* New York: AMACOM, 1982. 216 p.

This is a practical guide to operations of a customer service department that handles customer contacts from the placement of an order to the delivery of the item or services. Emphasis is on the support of the company's marketing efforts.

647. Bobrow, Edwin E., and Wizenberg, Larry, eds. *Sales Manager's Handbook.* Homewood, IL: Dow Jones-Irwin, 1983. 522 p.

This state-of-the-art manual is a collection of articles written by authorities on topics that are relevant to the sales manager. These include an overview of sales management responsibilities, methods of selling goods, productivity, sales campaigns, training, development and compensation of sales people, and the place of the sales force management in the company.

648. Bullus, Gerald E. *The Manager's Guide to Sales Incentives.* Aldershot, Hants, England: Gower, 1983. 148 p.

The use of incentives to motivate the sales force is an important part of a company's marketing plan. The roles of the sales manager in successfully promoting incentives is covered including objectives, checklists, and case histories.

649. Callanan, Joseph A., and Porter, Henry. *Sales Management and Motivation.* New York: Franklin Watts, 1987. 204 p.

This guide to creating an effective sales program begins with clearly stated objectives based on the company's needs. The development of the plan includes recruiting sales personnel, compensation for the sales force, preparing sales reports, sales forecasting, evaluating staff performance, creative training programs, and using sales meetings as motivators.

650. Calvin, Robert J. *Profitable Sales Management and Marketing for Growing Businesses.* New York: Van Nostrand, 1984. 376 p.

Practical, inexpensive, and proven techniques show the small business person, who is reponsible for sales management and marketing, how to capitalize on the strength of the business, while compensating for its weaknesses. Hiring, training, and motivating sales people; introduction of new products; pricing; advertising; and distribution are some of the areas covered.

651. Coughlin, Anne T., and Sen, Subrata K. *Salesforce Compensation: Insights from Management Science.* Cambridge, MA: Marketing Science Institute, 1986. 70 p.

Business people and academicians will find this survey of compensation plans useful. Areas covered include the identification of characteristics of firms, salespeople, the markets in which they sell and the compensation plans used, a review of the literature, and empirical evidence on salesforce compensation plans.

652. Cravens, David W. *The Sales Manager's Book of Marketing Planning.* Homewood, IL: Dow Jones-Irwin, Inc., 1983. 244 p.

The manager who wants a complete, yet concise, practical guide to developing a marketing plan is guided through the step-by-step process. Techniques for evaluating and refining the plan as well as guidelines for implementation are included. Checklists help in reviewing the market plan.

653. Dunn, Albert H., and Johnson, Eugene M. *Managing Your Sales Team.* Englewood Cliffs, NJ: Prentice-Hall, 1980. 256 p.

Using analytical checklists, self-quizzes, brain teasers, and thought provokers, the author challenges the sales manager to develop skills and insights. Planning, recruiting, selection, training, leadership and supervision, sales force incentives, and compensation and evaluation are the areas covered.

654. Friday, William. *How to Sell Your Product through (Not to) Wholesalers.* San Francisco, CA: Prudential Publishing Co., 1980. 208 p.

A practical handbook for the manufacturer who wants to develop this marketing channel. The pros and cons and difficulties are covered, along with information on selecting and working with the wholesaler and the salespeople, distribution rights, using brokers and manufacturers' agents, hiring, training, and compensating sales personnel. A list of definitions of the different persons involved in wholesaling is included.

655. Hancock, W. A., ed. *Guide to Purchase & Sales Forms.* Loose-leaf. Chesterfield, OH: Business Laws, 1984.
Included in this loose-leaf binder are practical forms for simple transactions and comprehensive forms for complex transactions. Most have explanations for the important points of the agreements. Examples of forms used by various companies and some ethics forms are provided.

656. Henry, Porter, and Callanan, Joseph A. *Sales Management and Motivation.* New York: Watts, 1987. 204 p.
A complete guide for creating an effective and profitable sales program covers the organization of the sales territories for cost-effective coverage, determination of the size of the staff for efficient operation, development of training and compensation programs, motivating and evaulating sales personnel.

657. Odiorne, George S. *Sales Management by Objectives: A Hands-on Management Guide to a Systematic Method for Increasing Sales and Profits.* Chicago: Dartnell Corp., 1982. 305 p.
This systematic approach for increasing sales and profits includes preparing a multiyear strategic plan, establishing specific objectives for each salesperson, locating sales growth opportunities and using techniques for successful market penetration.

658. Patty, C. Robert. *Sales Manager's Handbook.* Reston, VA: Reston Publishing Co., 1982. 468 p.
A how-to book for the new sales manager as well as the regional or national manager that illustrates ways of looking at controversial topics to identify the basic issues. Skill in managing sales personnel and the basics of selling are some areas covered.

659. Riso, Ovid, ed. *Sales Manager's Handbook.* 13th ed. Chicago: Dartnell Corp., 1980. 1,006 p.
The fundamentals of sales management are presented in this handbook designed to quickly provide information about developing the product or service, analyzing the market, channels of distribution, competitive sales practices, sales policies, and recruiting and training of the sales force. Specific examples of forms needed by sales managers are included.

660. Ryckman, W. G. *Compensating Your Sales Force.* Chicago: Probus Publishing Co., 1986. 227 p.
Designed for sales managers who are responsible for compensation plans for sales personnel, this book discusses the strengths and weaknesses of various methods of paying the sales force. Territories, quotas, sales expenses, contests, and policy decisions are also important for reaching the company's sales objectives.

661. Schlom, Charles C. *How to Plan and Manage Sales Territories Effectively.* Chicago: Dartnell Corp., 1974–.
A loose-leaf guide to help determine the market within a salesperson's territory, including the number of products or lines being sold and their acceptance, the number of customers in a territory and which of these can become a key account. This evaluation of territory potential contributes to the overall sales and profits of the company.

662. Seltz, David D. *How to Conduct Successful Sales Contests and Incentive Programs.* Chicago: Dartnell Corp., 1979. 353 p.

This manual covers proven incentive programs that motivate the sales force. Explanations of the different types of programs, including sales contests, dealer contests, wholesaler and jobber contests, are included.

663. Smith, Roger F. *Sales Management: A Practitioner's Guide.* Englewood Cliffs, NJ: Prentice-Hall, 1987. 261 p.

A primer approach for the sales manager of a large or small firm that describes the nature of the sales job and its role in marketing, covering basic principles for designing a sales program. Sales management is not a series of steps but involves interrelated skills and events.

664. Stumm, David Arthur. *Developing a Professional Sales Force: A Guide for Sales Trainers and Sales Managers.* New York: Quorum Books, 1986. 218 p.

Designed for the sales manager, this book provides information not only for those training sales personnel, but also for those who want to upgrade their sales skills. Theories behind sales skills are explained, and the author shows how these translate into specific sales applications and how these ideas can be used in training modules for a particular industry or product.

665. Wallis, Louis A. *Computers and the Sales Effort.* New York: The Conference Board, Inc., 1986. 26 p.

The nature, extent, and success of computerized sales-support systems and the experiences of selected companies in developing and using such systems is covered.

666. Webster, Frederick E., Jr. *Field Sales Management.* New York: Wiley, 1983. 249 p.

Intended for present and potential field sales managers, this book is not about selling or management. It concentrates on the direction and development of field sales personnel, who, along with sales representatives, are important in implementing marketing strategy. Of importance are the discussions of field sales representatives, the field sales manager, the buying process and buyer, and the seller interaction.

PAPERS—COLLECTED

667. Ford, Neil M.; Churchill, Gilbert A., Jr.; and Walker, Orville, C., Jr., eds. *Sales Force Performance.* Lexington, MA: Lexington Books, 1985. 306 p.

The major variables affecting a salesperson's performance that are included in the model of sales performance used in this volume are role perceptions, aptitude/skill level, and motivation and personal, organizational and environmental factors. Each section has an introduction to the concept, with an explanation of how the topics of the following articles are related to the concept.

PERIODICALS/ANNUALS

668. *Agency Sales: The Marketing Magazine for Manufacturers' Agencies and Their Principles.* Monthly. Laguna Hills, CA: Manufacturers' Agents National Assn.

For the executive of a sales agency, this trade publication provides information on topics such as market planning, sales motivation, trends in administration of a sales force, sales opportunities, management techniques, and a calendar of industry shows.

669. *Personal Selling Power.* Bimonthly. Fredericksburg, VA: Gerhard Gschwandtner & Associates.
An advisory publication for sales and marketing executives that contains explanations of successful sales techniques.

670. *Portfolio.* Annual. New York: Sales & Marketing Management.
This is an annual collection of successful plans for areas such as sales force management, sales training and recruiting, marketing research, advertising, marketing through an outside sales force, and time and territory management.

671. *Sales and Marketing Executive Report.* Biweekly. Chicago: Dartnell Corp.
This newsletter covers the latest developments in the sales/marketing field in capsulized format to help the busy executive review and evaluate business building programs and techniques.

672. *Sales & Marketing Management.* Monthly. New York: Bill Communications, Inc.
The most important magazine in this area covers ideas, techniques, trends, and predictions for such areas as sales promotion, test marketing, managing costs, telemarketing, sales training and recruiting, performance, motivation, and compensation. Four special issues are *Survey of Selling Costs* (February issue), *Survey of Industrial & Commercial Buying Power* (April issue), and the two-part series of *Survey of Buying Power* (July and October issues) covering consumer and retail statistical information.

673. *Sales Manager's Bulletin.* Bimonthly. Waterford, CT: National Sales Development Institute.
Concise articles cover topics such as recruiting and hiring, new marketing ideas, competitive strategies, incentive systems, sales techniques, training suggestions, and marketing research.

STATISTICAL INFORMATION

674. *Dartnell's Sales Force Compensation.* Biannual. Chicago: Dartnell Corp.
Statistical data from more than 300 U.S. and Canadian companies employing more than 15,000 salespeople provide information on earnings by industry, compensation plans, expense allowances, fringe benefits, and incentive plans. The cost effectiveness of various plans is also covered.

675. *Survey of Selling Costs.* Annual. New York: Sales & Marketing Management.
This compilation of selling facts and figures includes the "Selling Cost Index" and "Cost Per Sales Call" estimates for leading metro markets. The markets with the highest and lowest sales costs are noted. The information helps in determining and controlling selling expenses such as sales training, meetings, travel and entertainment, and other sales-support activities.

ASSOCIATIONS

Association of Sales Administration Managers. P.O. Box 737, Harrison, NJ 07029.
Sales Executives Club of New York. 114 E. 32nd St., New York, NY 10016.

Sales Promotion

DIRECTORIES

676. *Directory of Incentive Sources.* Annual. New York: Bill Communications, Inc.

An annual issue of the journal *Incentive Marketing* that lists product supplies for promotional incentives and premiums that are used in conducting premium or incentive advertising campaigns. An index by service or product is included.

677. *Directory of Premiums, Incentives and Travel Buyers.* Annual. New York: Salesman's Guide, Inc.

Formerly the *Directory of Premium and Incentive Buyers,* this annual lists the individuals responsible for buying premiums, incentives, and incentive travel.

678. *Premium/Incentive Business Directory of Premium Suppliers and Services Issue.* Annual. New York: Gralla Publications.

Almost 2,000 manufacturers, categorized by product, are listed. The section on incentives reps and consultants gives details of territories served and incentive travel supplies and services.

GUIDEBOOKS/HANDBOOKS

679. Bowman, Russell D. *Profit on the Dotted Line: Coupons and Rebates.* 2d ed. Chicago: Commerce Communicatins, Inc., 1985. 230 p.

For the novice as well as the expert, this edition covers new strategies and techniques, including the impact of technology. The first section is an overview complete with explanations of basic techniques and how to use them in the total marketing mix. The second section covers coupons, planning and testing, estimating redemption rates, fraud, and their use by restaurants and other service organizations. The third section gives information on the use of refunds and rebates, including estimating and use of fulfillment houses.

680. Feinman, Jeffrey P.; Blashek, Robert D.; and McCabe, Richard J. *Sweepstakes, Prize Promotions, Games and Contests.* Homewood, IL: Dow Jones-Irwin, 1986. 180 p.

Although essentially for marketing people, this book is useful for any business that wants to increase sales and gain market share or a position of leadership by offering something consumers do not expect. Included are types of prize promotions, what they can and cannot do, guidelines for planning, the use of various media for promotion, the legal aspects, and the future of such promotions.

681. Foote, Cameron S. *The Fourth Medium: How to Use Promotional Literature to Increase Sales and Profits.* Homewood, IL: Dow Jones-Irwin, 1986. 226 p.

Promotional literature can have an impact on marketing success, and this book covers every aspect of preparation and production from developing the concept to distribution.

682. Herpel, George L., and Slack, Steve. *Specialty Advertising: New Dimensions in Creative Marketing.* Irving, TX: Specialty Advertising Assn., International, 1983. 188 p.

A scholarly and practical approach provide a perspective on specialty advertising, what it is, how and when to use it. Areas covered include the promotional mix, behavioral factors, promotion evaluation, developing image, motivating deals, and building and maintaining market share.

683. Rapp, Stan, and Collins, Thomas L. *Maximarketing: The New Direction in Promotion, Advertising & Marketing Strategy.* New York: McGraw-Hill, 1986. 256 p.

The nine sequential steps common to all forms of marketing to the consumer are illustrated with examples that make advertising more cost effective, show how to locate prime prospects, develop repeat sales, discover profitable new media, and present distribution channels that reflect the changes in the way goods and services are advertised and promoted. Checklists and models are included.

684. Riso, Ovid. *Sales Promotion Handbook.* 7th ed. Chicago: Dartnell Corp., 1979. 1,206 p.

A practical compilation that explains ideas, methods, and techniques for developing and evaluating the success of a sales promotion plan. Coverage includes organization, budgeting, sales leads, customer service, trade shows, motivating salespeople, and public relations. Examples, illustrations, and charts are supplied. Lists of business directories and publications are a part of this desk reference handbook.

685. Schultz, Don E., and Robinson, William A. *Sales Promotion Essentials.* Chicago: Crain Books, 1982. 234 p.

Descriptions of practical and proven sales promotion techniques and how to include them in the marketing mix to achieve the best results are discussed. The sales promotions that are explained are coupons, contests or sweepstakes, bonus packs, stamp plans, price-offs, refund offers, trade coupons, trade allowances, and sampling. The strengths and weaknesses of each are noted, and the criteria for choosing any one for a specific marketing problem are provided.

686. Seltz, David D. *Handbook of Innovative Marketing Techniques.* Reading, MA: Addison-Wesley, 1981. 329 p.

Techniques for achieving maximum market coverage with a minimum of capital outlays are covered in this book. These include sales-generating concepts such as the party plan, marketing off premises, fund raising ideas, using premiums, and the rental concept.

687. Strang, Roger A. *The Promotional Planning Process.* New York: Praeger, 1980. 127 p.

This book describes and models the decision process for promotional planning and budgeting in consumer goods manufacturing companies. The factors that influence the importance of advertising and sales promotion in relation to brand marketing strategy are also covered.

688. Ulanoff, Stanley M., ed. *Handbook of Sales Promotion.* New York: McGraw-Hill, 1985. 607 p.

The many incentives used to promote consumer products are covered in this handbook. These include coupons, refunds, sweepstakes, sampling, and trading stamps. The technique of manufacturer's sales promotion to retailers, distributors, and the sales force are covered. Management aspects are also included for this growing method of sales promotion.

PAPERS—COLLECTED

689. Jocz, Katherine E., ed. *Research on Sales Promotion: Collected Papers.* Cambridge, MA: Marketing Science Institute, 1984. 123 p.

Academic research aimed at understanding the basic determinants of effective sales promotion can contribute to sales promotion management. These papers cover areas such as consumer response, consumer promotion, consumer motivation, ratios of promotion and advertising to sales, and symbiotic sales promotion.

690. Mahany, Gene. *Mahany on Sales Promotion.* Chicago: Crain Books, 1982. 125 p.

A collection of articles from the author's column in *Advertising Age* that covers general trends, consumer and trade promotions, techniques, and product promotions.

PERIODICALS

691. *Creative: The Magazine of Promotion and Marketing.* Bimonthly. New York: Magazines Creative, Inc.

Articles cover a variety of topics for sales promotions and merchandising with additional information in areas such as new logos and trademarks, licensing, new research studies, exhibit surveys, direct marketing, trade shows, and incentives.

692. *Incentive Marketing.* Monthly. New York: Bill Communications, Inc.

Articles cover merchandise and travel incentives for dealers and salespeople. Consumer promotions such as gifts, premiums, coupons, and sweepstakes/contests are also covered. An annual statistical feature reports on incentive spending by industry.

693. *Premium Incentive Business: The National Newsmagazine for Promotion Marketing.* Monthly. New York: Gralla Publications.

News, trends, legislation, product reviews, promotions and incentives used by various companies, incentive travel, trade shows, new products, and a list of new catalogs are some areas covered.

PROCEEDINGS

694. Farley, John U. Executive Director. *Measuring and Evaluating Sales Promotions to the Trade and to Consumers: Summary of MSI Conference.* Cambridge, MA: Marketing Science Institute, 1985. unpaged.

The papers presented at this conference used model approaches for various types of sales promotions such as coupons, trade deals, or retailer promotions and the type of effect these had on sales.

ASSOCIATIONS

Council of Sales Promotion Agencies. 2130 Delancey Pl., Philadelphia, PA 19103.

National Premium Sales Executives, Inc. 1600 Rts. 22, Union, NJ 07083.

Premium Industry Club. P.O. Box 2098, Schiller, Park, IL 60176.

Promotion Marketing Assn. of America. 322 Eighth Ave., Suite 1201, New York, NY 10036.

Specialty Advertising Association International. 1404 Walnut Hill Lane, Irving, TX 75038.

Services Marketing

BIBLIOGRAPHIES

695. Fisk, Raymond P., and Tansuhaj, Patriya S. *Services Marketing: An Annotated Bibliography.* Chicago: American Marketing Assn., 1985. 256 p.

More than twenty-one years of literature, from 1964–1983, included in this bibliography covering journal articles, conference proceedings, books, and dissertations. The 1,991 entries are arranged in two parts. Conceptual insights include areas such as foundation, marketing strategy for services, elements in the service mix, and management issues. Part two is about ten service fields such as health care, financial, professional, travel and tourism, sports, and educational and telecommunication services.

GUIDEBOOKS/HANDBOOKS

696. Gronroos, Christian. *Strategic Management and Marketing in the Service Sector.* rev. ed. Cambridge, MA: Marketing Science Institute, 1983. 120 p.

For the service firm, this publication develops a theory of strategic management and marketing of services that is both profit and market oriented.

697. Holtz, Herman. *Marketing with Seminars and Newsletters.* Westport, CT: Greenwood Press, 1986. 227 p.

High-tech and professional service industries require different marketing approaches. Instead of slogans, sales letters, brochures, and catalogs, the use of information transfer techniques is preferable. This handbook is a guide to these techniques for sophisticated goods and services. Organization, production, costs, testing, and sources of support services are covered.

698. Johnson, Eugene M.; Scheuing, Eberhard E.; and Gaida, Kathleen A. *Profitable Service Marketing.* Homewood, IL: Dow Jones-Irwin, 1986. 303 p.

Intended for the service manager, this book analyzes the nature of service, the service environment, the management cycle, and the service marketing mix. Major issues and trends that confront the manager and the practical application of modern marketing concepts and practices are covered.

699. McCaffrey, Mike, and Derloshon, Jerry. *Personal Marketing Strategies: How to Sell Yourself, Your Ideas, and Your Services.* New York: Prentice-Hall, 1983. 219 p.

The four phases of personal marketing of professional services involve creating a public image through a variety of means, developing relationships, the selling phase, and retaining clients. Each of these is clearly explained with worksheets and forms. Sample letters and a short list of books on this subject are included.

PERIODICALS

700. *Journal of Professional Services Marketing.* Quarterly. New York: Haworth Press, Inc.
Practical marketing tools for specific service sectors of the economy and the latest marketing issues and methodologies in the service industry are covered. This includes banking, financial services, consulting, law, telecommunications, insurance, social services, hotels, and restaurants.

701. *Journal of Service Marketing.* Quarterly. Santa Barbara, CA: Grayson Associates.
Articles are based on case studies, research or business practices and are aimed at the professional marketer and the academician. Areas covered include new concepts or ideas and can be considered contributions to the literature.

702. *Services Marketing Newsletter.* Quarterly. Chicago: American Marketing Assn.
Articles cover new ideas, trends, service marketing theories, and case histories and are written by professionals in the field, including both business practitioners and educators.

PROCEEDINGS

703. Berry, Leonard L.; Shostack, G. Lynn; and Upah, Gregory D., eds. *Emerging Perspectives on Services Marketing.* Chicago: American Marketing Assn., 1985. 146 p.
The papers cover a variety of topics including consumer evaluation processes, consumer satisfaction, issues in new service development, research priorities in services marketing, and implementing services marketing.

704. Bloch, Thomas M., et al., eds. *Services Marketing in a Changing Environment.* Chicago: American Marketing Assn., 1985. 138 p.
A collection of papers from top executives in the leading service industries who presented solutions to problems of the changing regulatory and competitive environment. Also includes papers on consumer behavior, marketing theory, and research.

705. Donnelly, James H., and George, William R., eds. *Marketing of Services.* Chicago: American Marketing Assn., 1981. 244 p.
This is a collection of papers presented at the first AMA conference which focused on this topic. Various aspects of commercial, professional, and nonprofit/public sector service marketing and service theory are covered.

706. George, William R., and Marshall, Claudia E. *Developing New Services.* Chicago: American Marketing Assn., 1984. 112 p.
The papers presented at this symposium focus on the marketing of services. The three basic areas are the development of a climate for innovation of new services, systems and processes for new services development, and the role of employees in this process.

707. Venkatesan, Diane M., and Schmalensee, Claudia Marshall. *Creativity in Services Marketing: What's New, What Works, What's Developing.* Chicago: American Marketing Assn., 1986. 175 p.
The papers cover areas such as managing service marketing, understanding the service customer, corporate culture and internal marketing, industry-specific topics, and research issues.

STATISTICAL INFORMATION

708. U.S. Bureau of the Census. *Census of Service Industries.* Every 5 years. Washington, DC: U.S. Government Printing Office.
Data on almost 130 service industries such as hotels, law firms, and amusement and recreation services are presented in two volumes by industry and geographical areas. Statistics cover number of establishments, payroll, and employment. Preliminary issues are published and cumulated in the final volumes.

ASSOCIATIONS

Society for Marketing Professional Services. 801 N. Fairfax St., Suite 215, Alexandria, VA 22314.

FINANCIAL SERVICES MARKETING

Bibliographies

709. *Annotated Bibliography of Secondary Sources for Bank Marketing Research.* Chicago: Information Center, Bank Marketing Assn., 1986. 28 p.
Data sources, fact books, directories, special issues of periodicals, and federal and local government information are included. Useful for locating statistical information, writing a marketing plan, and determining market share or competitive analysis.

Databases

710. FINIS: Financial Industry Information Service. 1982–. Chicago: Bank Marketing Assn. (Vendors: BRS, DIAL, MEAD).
Provides marketing information on organizations in the financial services community and on products and services for corporate and retail customers.

Guidebooks/Handbooks

711. Benn, Alec. *Advertising Financial Products and Services: Proven Techniques and Principles for Banks, Investment Firms, Insurance Companies and Their Agencies.* Westport, CT: Quorum Books, 1986. 231 p.
Authoritve guidance for both the beginner and the professional covers creative strategy, copywriting, art direction, media selection, and legal regulations. Principles and techniques are explained, and time-saving checklists are included.

712. Berry, Leonard L.; Futrell, Charles M.; and Bowers, Michael R. *Bankers Who Sell: Improving Selling Effectiveness in Banking.* Chicago: Bank Marketing Assn.; Homewood, IL: Dow Jones-Irwin, 1985. 158 p.
Intended for both large and small banks interested in selling to the commercial or retail markets, this book provides a framework for the development of a sales program. The topics covered include defining the sales task, selecting and training sales personnel, facilitating selling, and measuring and rewarding sales performance.

713. McMahon, Robert J. *Bank Marketing Handbook: How to Compete in the Financial Services Industry.* Boston: Bank Publishing Co., 1986. 339 p.
> A guide to productive methods and techniques for marketing products and services of commercial banks. Includes charts, worksheets, and checklists, most of which are easily programmed for personal computers or mainframes.

714. Moebs, G. Michael, and Moebs, Eva. *Pricing Financial Services.* Homewood, IL: Dow Jones-Irwin, 1986. 246 p.
> Theory, practices, and specific tools are combined to provide a method for properly pricing financial services. Pricing principles, price strategies, and implementing prices are the broad topics which have many subtopics such as cost considerations, laws, regulations, and the methodology for implementing prices.

715. Motley, L. Biff. *Pricing Deposit Services: A Decision Making Handbook.* Boston: Banker's Publishing Co., 1983. 217 p.
> General pricing fundamentals are applied to checking, NOW, and savings accounts and Certificates of Deposit, focusing on costs, revenues break-even points, net income computation, and likely losses. Monitoring other institutions' services and costs are also covered in this step-by-step guide.

716. *A Practical Guide to Market Research.* Rolling Meadows, IL: Bank Administration Institute, 1982. 45 p.
> Written for the individual with little experience in conducting market research, this manual is a guide for bank personnel designing and carrying out marketing research. Planning, issues involved in sample selection, designing a questionnaire, guidelines for scheduling and budgeting, and telephone interviewing techniques are some of the topics covered.

717. Reidenbach, R. Eric, and Grubbs, M. Ray. *Developing New Banking Products: A Manager's Guide.* New York: Prentice-Hall, 1986. 206 p.
> New product development for banks, regardless of size, is detailed in this book which concentrates on financial products. A practical, realistic approach is used to detail key elements of idea generation, screening, concept development, and testing.

718. Richardson, Linda. *Bankers in the Selling Role: A Consultative Guide to Cross-Selling Financial Services.* 2d ed. New York: Wiley, 1984. 177 p.
> Proven ideas for successful commercial calling efforts are explained. These ideas can improve personal calling skills and aid in the bank's planning efforts for selling to the commercial market.

719. Winston, William J., ed. *Marketing for Financial Services.* New York: Haworth Press, Inc., 1986. 143 p.
> Originally published as *Journal of Professional Services Marketing* vol. 1, no. 3 (Spring 1986), this reprint publication covers strategic marketing planning, customer approach, direct marketing, pricing, attitudinal and behavioral characteristics of consumer groups, and marketing within a firm.

Periodicals

720. *Bank Marketing: Publication of the Bank Marketing Assn.* Monthly. Chicago: The Association.
> Articles on marketing techniques that are useful to the banking industry cover a wide variety of topics. Examples of advertising campaigns are included. The July issue contains a "Directory of Bank Marketing Services" categorized for ease in locating supplies.

721. *Bank Marketing Report.* Monthly. Boston: Warren, Gorham & Lamont.
A monthly publication for bank executives covering examples of successful marketing of bank services. Reports on various topics such as methods of attracting customers, direct mail, marketing dual credit cards, new ideas on savings clubs, and opportunities for cross-selling are included.

722. *Journal of Retail Banking.* Quarterly. Arlington, VA: Consumer Bankers Assn.
The practices of retail banking are the focus of this journal which emphasizes practical methods, concepts, and current research issues covering management, interest rates, deposits, consumer credit, and regulatory issues.

Associations

Bank Marketing Assn. 309 W. Washington St., Chicago, IL 60606.
Financial Institutions Marketing Assn. 111 E. Wacker Dr., Chicago, IL 60601.
Financial Marketing Assn. 6320 Monona Dr., Suite 300, Madison, WI 53716.

HEALTH CARE MARKETING

Bibliographies

723. Cooper, Philip D.; Jones, Karen M.; and Wong, John K. *An Annotated and Extended Bibliography of Health Care Marketing.* Chicago: American Marketing Assn., 1984. 186 p.
More than 600 articles, published from the late 1970s through 1984 are included in this bibliography. Double cross-references list an article by the marketing area such as market research or service development and also by the health care setting such as a hospital or nursing home.

Directories

724. *The Medical and Healthcare Marketplace Guide: A Comprehensive Industrial Guide to the U.S. Medical and Health Care Marketplace.* Annual. Miami, FL: International Bio-Medical Information Service.
Detailed profiles of more than 4,400 public and private medical and health-related companies, including foreign-owned companies and subsidiaries, are listed. These cover manufacturers, dealers, distributors, importers, and exporters in 247 separate product/service classifications. Sales and market shares for the fifty product and services areas and rankings for the top 500 largest companies are included.

Guidebooks/Handbooks

725. Cooper, Philip D. *Health Care Marketing: Issues and Trends.* 2d ed. Rockville, MD: Aspen Systems Corp., 1985. 450 p.
A guide to successful strategies and how to apply them to the health care setting, this is a collection of forty-six selected articles, some of which are classics, others discuss what's best in the new literature.

726. Kotler, Philip, and Clarke, Roberta N. *Marketing for Health Care Organizations.* 2d ed. Englewood Cliffs, NJ: Prentice-Hall, 1987. 545 p.
The conceptual systems of marketing are applied to the marketing problems of health care and social service organizations. Organizing market research, analyzing market opportunities, planning the marketing mix, and support of the marketing effort are covered.

727. Rothman, Jack, et al. *Marketing Human Service Innovations.* Beverly Hills, CA: Sage Publications, 1983. 271 p.
Intended for professionals in the mental health field, this book includes techniques and strategies for dealing with organizational and community aspects of this field. Areas included are the mass communication approach, the interpersonal approach, and the implications of social marketing.

728. Skinner, Patricia. *Marketing Community Health Services.* New York: National League for Nursing, 1979. 42 p.
The use of marketing techniques is explained in relation to the marketing of home health services. Planning, communication, and recommendations are included.

729. Winston, William J., ed. *Advertising Handbook for Health Care Services.* New York: Haworth Press, 1986. 287 p.
This book is aimed at the marketing practitioner and administrator of health care organizations. Practical suggestions for developing effective advertising, including examples of excellent advertising, that is a cost-effective marketing tool, are presented. Developing an effective and productive relationship with an advertising agency is also discussed.

730. Winston, William J. *How to Write a Marketing Plan for Health Care Organizations.* New York: Haworth Press, Inc., 1985. 170 p.
Health care administrators should focus on the marketplace, and this guide covers the basic steps in the market planning process which can be used in hospitals, group practices, clinics, and other types of health facilities.

731. Winston, William J. *Marketing the Group Practice: Practical Methods for the Health Care Practitioner.* New York: Haworth Press, Inc., 1983. 107 p.
The techniques demonstrated are applicable to a variety of health providers such as physicians, dentists, optometrists, veternarians, and others. Tips on working with consultants, developing a plan of action, public relations, information collection, and recruiting colleagues are some of the areas covered. This was also published as the *Health Marketing Quarterly,* vol. 1 (Fall 1983).

Periodicals

732. *Changing Medical Markets.* Monthly. Waterfield, CT: Theta Technology Corp.
Aimed at the medicial devices and diagnostic products market, this publication has information on new products, company reports, news on current and foreign research, and analysis of the impact of products on the market.

733. *Health Marketing Quarterly.* Quarterly. New York: Haworth Press, Inc.
Each issue is devoted to a different health or human service or delivery system. The articles, from educators and practitioners, provide the administrators of health care with a framework for assisting them in marketing their services.

734. *Healthcare Marketing Report: The National Newspaper of Healthcare Marketing.* Monthly. Atlanta, GA: Healthcare Marketing Report.
Articles cover methods used by various health care agencies to advertise and promote their services. Examples of advertising campaigns, news items, and brief statistical information are included.

735. *Journal of Health Care Marketing.* Quarterly. Chicago: American Marketing Assn.
For the practitioner and the academic, this journal is a bridge between the developing of marketing theories and the practical application of these theories to the various areas of health care marketing. Abstracts of pertinent articles on health care marketing are also included.

736. *Journal of Pharmaceutical Marketing & Management.* Quarterly. New York: Haworth Press, Inc.
The articles cover the problems of management and marketing products and services in manufacuturing and wholesaling for the pharmaceutical industry. Institutional and academic components are also included.

737. *Medical Marketing & Media.* Monthly. Boca Raton, FL: CPS Communications, Inc.
Articles cover legislation, recent happenings in the industry, new products, developments, trends, and predictions of marketing significance. An annual and midyear "Market Facts" review provides information on industry promotion activities, use of the sales force, new technology, and media.

738. *MPS: Medical Product Sales.* Monthly. Northfield, IL: McKnight Medical Communications Co.
The official journal of the Health Industry Distribution Association, this monthly publication covers products for the entire health care marketplace. Trends, legislation, marketing mergers, and management are some topics covered. New products are listed in each issue.

Proceedings

739. Cooper, Philip D., ed. *Responding to the Challenge: Health Care Marketing Comes of Age.* Chicago: American Marketing Assn., 1986. 180 p.
The papers at the Sixth Annual Symposium on Health Services Marketing are grouped by financial aspects, new product development, marketing channels, communications, marketing information systems, and building an effective organization.

740. Paul, D. Terry, ed. *Building Marketing Effectiveness in Health Care: A Proceedings.* Chicago: American Marketing Assn., 1985. 169 p.
Papers presented at the Fifth Annual Symposium on Health Services Marketing cover marketing principles as they apply to health care, advertising, marketing, research, and marketing of alternative health services.

Associations

American College of Healthcare Marketing. 5530 Wisconsin Ave., N.W., Suite 917, Washington, DC 20815.
Health Industry Distributors Assn. 1701 Pennsylvania Ave., N.W., Suite 470, Washington, DC 20006.

NONPROFIT/PUBLIC MARKETING

Dictionaries

741. Ott, J. Steven, and Shafritz, Jay M. *Facts on File Dictionary of Nonprofit Organization Management.* New York: Facts on File, 1986. 407 p.
Words, terms, phrases, processes, laws, and court cases as they apply to nonprofit organizations are included in the dictionary. This covers areas such as accounting, business practices, labor relations, management theory, marketing, and public relations.

Guidebooks/Handbooks

742. Coffman, Larry L. *Public-Sector Marketing: A Guide for Practitioners.* New York: Wiley, 1986. 191 p.
This guide provides keys to organization structure, and fundamentals of planning, including research, methods of implementation, and performance evaluation. The marketing audit checklist provides a means of initiating or improving a marketing program.

743. Crompton, John L., and Lamb, Charles W., Jr. *Marketing Government and Social Services.* New York: Wiley, 1986. 485 p.
The purpose of this book is to present a general orientation to the field of marketing, to present new ideas for solving problems, and to provide a frame of reference for service delivery decisions. This information is directed at managers at all levels of government and all sizes of jurisdictions.

744. Kotler, Philip, and Andreasen, Alan R. *Strategic Marketing for Nonprofit Organizations.* 3d ed. Englewood Cliffs, NJ: Prentice-Hall, 1987. 560 p.
This book applies the conceptual system of marketing to the marketing problems of nonprofit organizations. In part one, the environment, the philosophy, and the basic concepts for targeting customer markets are discussed. Part two emphasizes strategic planning and organization. Part three covers conceptual tools for implementing detailed tactics and programs including the marketing mix.

745. Rados, David L. *Marketing for Non-Profit Organizations.* Boston: Auburn House Publishing Co., 1981. 572 p.
Intended for those associated with nonprofit organizations, this book is about the marketing problems that arise in charities, nonprofit businesses, labor unions, foundations, and research agencies. These problems include costs, giving, distribution, communication, marketing strategy, control, and organization.

746. Rubright, Robert, and McDonald, Dan. *Marketing Health & Human Services.* Rockville, MD: Aspen Systems Corp., 1981. 248 p.
A how-to publication that can be used by a variety of nonprofit organizations that trade in services, causes, behavioral changes, or education. Based on nine components that include selection of project, research, market audit, setting objectives, targeting, strategies, special promotional tools, internal adjustments, and evaluation/recycling, the author traces the development of a marketing plan.

747. Ruffner, Robert H. *Handbook of Publicity and Public Relations for the Nonprofit Organization.* Englewood Cliffs, NJ: Prentice-Hall, 1984. 247 p.
Nonprofit organizations can learn how to broaden their base of support and generate additional income. Low-cost, but high impact, public communication programs include sample forms and publicity materials for conveying the message to funding

sources, those receiving the organization's services, and the community. Research tools, strategies, and techniques help to set objectives, define problems, and suggest solutions.

Papers—Collected

748. Powell, Walter W., ed. *The Nonprofit Sector: A Research Handbook.* New Haven, CT: Yale University Press, 1987. 464 p.

A review and assessment of scholarly research in this area presents a realistic appraisal of current knowledge and pinpoints problems and areas needing additional research. Topics covered include the relationship of the volunteer sector to government and private enterprise, organizational and management issues, core functions, and financing issues.

Periodicals/Annuals

749. *Advances in Nonprofit Marketing.* Annual. Greenwich, CT: JAI Press, Inc., 1985.

Of interest to academicians and marketers, this collection of scholarly papers, longer than an article but not monographic in length, covers various aspects of nonprofit marketing.

PROFESSIONAL SERVICES MARKETING

Guidebooks/Handbooks

750. Congram, Carole A., and Dumesic, Ruth J. *The Accountant's Strategic Marketing Guide.* New York: Wiley, 1986. 193 p.

This is a comprehensive guide to making better decisions for marketing accounting services. By bringing together marketing activites such as publications, seminars, and public relations, the organization can have a coordinated strategy.

751. Connor, Richard A., and Davidson, Jeffrey P. *Marketing Your Consulting and Professional Services.* New York: Wiley, 1985. 219 p.

A step-by-step guide for creating a marketing plan which is based on a client-centered approach. Targeting the market, selling in person, direct mail, brochures, and ads in the local press are some of the areas covered.

752. Coxe, Weld. *Marketing Architectural and Engineering Services.* 2d ed. New York: Van Nostrand Reinhold, 1983. 272 p.

A comprehensive marketing plan and organization strategies use a step-by-step approach that shows how to research new business markets, identify prospective clients, prepare written and oral presentation, negotiate, and close commissions. The use of brochures, direct mail, and other advertising techniques are explained.

753. Denny, Robert W. *How to Market Legal Services.* New York: Van Nostrand Reinhold, 1984. 278 p.

The successful marketing techniques that are useful in today's competitive market include developing the market plan, establishing market segmentation, and initiating client review programs, public relations, and advertising.

754. Denny, Robert W. *Marketing Accounting Services.* New York: Van Nostrand Reinhold, 1983. 269 p.

The development of effective marketing plans for individual practitioners, local firms, and multioffice operations include a wide range of marketing techniques, traditional as well as the most modern. Public relations, advertising, sales promotion, use of seminars and conventions, and effective use of the telephone are included.

755. Hameroff, Eugene J., and Nichols, Sandra S. *How to Guarantee Professional Success: 715 Tested, Proven Techniques for Promoting Your Practice.* Washington, DC: Bermont Books, Inc., 1982. 183 p.

In this handbook, publicity and public relations are explained and the techniques for using these are covered including explanations for professional services marketing. Paid advertising information includes a media checklist, budgeting, writing copy, media strategy, and evaluating effectiveness of this method.

756. Henry, Donald L. *The Profitable Professional Practice.* Englewood Cliffs, NJ: Prentice-Hall, 1985. 286 p.

Techniques for a more profitable professional practice for a number of professions are covered in this guide. Information provided will help reduce workload, and increase productivity as well as increase income. Some areas covered include office administration, site selection, expanding the practice, organizing a professional corporation, legal rights, and tax information. Forms, tables, and planning charts are provided.

757. Jones, Gerre L. *How to Market Professional Design Services.* 2d ed. New York: McGraw-Hill, 1983. 338 p.

The principles and psychology of marketing are outlined along with suggestions for organizing a marketing plan, locating prospect sources, effective prospect qualification, indirect and direct communications, preparing and presenting proposals, and selling to the government.

758. Jones, Gerre L. *Public Relations for the Design Professional.* New York: McGraw-Hill, 1980. 278 p.

The proven and productive techniques of public relations cover tools, special events, audiovisuals, press releases, photography do's and don'ts, and internal and external publications. Methods for measuring results are included.

759. Mahon, James J. *The Marketing of Professional Accounting Services: A Personal Practice Development Approach.* 2d ed. New York: Wiley, 1982. 199 p.

Techniques and methods for acquiring new clients for solo practitioners and small firms as well as useful information for orienting staff members of large firms are included. These detailed and structured approaches are useful for the traditional firm interested in professional image.

760. Ronald, Mana M. *Successfully Developing Your Accounting Practice.* New York: Wiley, 1987. 314 p.

Whether starting a new firm or looking for ways to improve the income of an established company, this book is a how-to guide that offers proven marketing ideas and techniques that can help find clients and sell services. Included are ways to obtain prospects, develop direct mail, and use telemarketing, seminars, and newsletters for developing a model marketing plan.

761. Webb, Stanley G. *Marketing & Strategic Planning for Professional Service Firms.* New York: AMACOM, 1982. 293 p.
This book emphasizes marketing principles and techniques that monitor and analyze the company's environment and client perceptions. The planning, organizing, controlling, and communicating functions of management are covered as they apply to professional service firms.

Periodicals

762. *CPA Marketing Report.* Monthly. Atlanta, GA: Robert A. Palmer.
New, practical developments throughout the country are included along with the successful marketing techniques used by CPA firms.

TECHNICAL MARKETING

Directories

763. Hoffman, Roger. *The Complete Software Marketplace 1984-85.* New York: Warner Books, 1984. 236 p.
Included in this directory are software buying companies, distributors, venture capital firms, lawyers with computer law experience, industry publications, consultants, market research organizations, and other individuals and groups who can assist the novice trying to market software.

764. *MMP: Microcomputer Marketplace: The Comprehensive Directory of the Microcomputer Industry.* Annual. New York: Bowker.
Listings include software publishers, magazines and newsletters, consultants, software developers, market researchers, and a variety of companies providing products and services in this industry. Nineteen indexes are provided for locating specific information.

765. Smolin, Ronald P., and Pickard, Thomas Michael. *Computer Industry: A Directory and Ranking of Public Companies.* Annual. Philadelphia, PA: AIIS.
Profiles and rankings of more than 700 public companies that manufacture computer systems, peripherals, data communications devices, and product software; provide computer services; and sell computer products. The companies are arranged by computer sectors, rankings are by market value and by sales, and an alphabetical listing is provided.

766. *Technology Transfer Directory: A Guide to Brokers, Seekers, Sellers, Facilitators, Databases, Directories, Organizations and Bibliographies in the Field of Technology Transfer.* Paoli, PA: GRQ, 1986. 330 p.
This directory provides information for anyone wanting to license, buy, market, or otherwise transfer technology between organizations. Sections on industries, universities, brokers, state and local development agencies, and research institutes provide additional information.

Guidebooks/Handbooks

767. David, Robert E. *Selling Your Software: A Beginner's Guide to Developing and Marketing Basic Software.* New York: Wiley, 1985. 140 p.

Section one covers programming, including basics such as choosing a topic, selecting a computer, and sample programs. Section two is about selling a program directly, commercial program marketing, copyrights, contracts, and after the sale. A reference manual for BASIC is also included.

768. Davidow, William H. *Marketing High Technology: An Insiders View.* New York: Free Press, 1986. 194 p.

The differences of marketing high technology products as compared with consumer products is explained. The importance of marketing strategy, need for international markets, provision of services, and pricing are some of the topics in this book.

769. Goldmacher, Irving. *Selling Microcomputers and Software.* New York: McGraw-Hill, 1985. 236 p.

The author looks at the unlimited market for these products and includes basic information about them, defines the major markets and the five areas of business for making a choice for the mode of business preferred. The successful strategies, skills, and techniques are outlined and provide practical advice that can be applied to the corporate, institutional, or retail environment.

770. Joyce, Dennis, and Pickering, John Earl. *The Software Writer's Market-Place.* Philadelphia, PA: Running Press Book Publishers, 1984. 160 p.

For the individual interested in marketing software that he/she has developed, this guide explains the process covering topics such as salability, user manuals, copyrighting, and submission guidelines. A list of companies to contact, text of a typical contract, and a cross-index of software applications are included.

771. Nisen, William G.; Schmidt, Allan; and Alterman, Ira. *Marketing Your Software: 26 Steps to Success.* Reading, MA: Addison-Wesley, 1984. 218 p.

This workbook is for software authors, entrepreneurs, and programmers. Each action step taken is to be recorded on worksheets at the end of the step which, when completed, is a detailed marketing plan covering areas such as potential trends, preparation of software for the market, costs to deliver the program, and when to begin thinking about second-generation products.

772. Shanklin, William L., and Ryans, John K. *Essentials of Marketing High Technology.* rev. ed. Lexington, MA: Lexington Books, 1986. 353 p.

This book is aimed at the professional as well as the student who is interested in what to do to successfully market high technology. It concentrates on the supply-side marketing concept rather than demand-side marketing with tighter marketing and R&D linkages.

773. Thatcher, Ance W. *Fast Forward: Planning for High Technology Marketing.* Windham, NH: Ballantrae Technical Books, 1985.

A step-by-step guide, with work sheets, that covers positioning, objectives, strategies, sales, costs, and profits for an industry that relies on applied scientific knowledge and engineering skills.

774. Wynne, Michael P. *Sci-Tech Selling: Selling Scientific and Technical Products and Services.* New York: Prentice-Hall, 1987. 217 p.

Selling scientific and technical products and services is a complex task because of the applications and situations into which they must be fitted, especially in large organizations. To help the sales person develop skills in this area, each chapter is a series of exercises to practice the concepts presented. These include research, contacts, problem identification, problem solving, closing, price, negotiations, and follow-up.

Periodicals

775. *Computer & Electronics Marketing.* Monthly. New York: A/S/M Communications.
Interpretive news reports, case histories, analysis of trends, and market strategy are included in this tabloid format.

776. *Electronic Market Trends.* Monthly. Washington, DC: Electronic Industries Assn.
Articles cover new products, applications, trends in employment, sales, selected product categories, and market sectors. Statistical tables have data on areas such as market opportunities, competition, foreign direct investment, and trends in computers.

777. *High Tech Marketing.* Monthly. Westport, CT: Technical Marketing Co.
The journal includes information on industry trends, marketing techniques, analysis, and implementation of marketing strategies. New products or academically oriented material are not covered. Aimed at senior marketing executives in the high technology industry.

778. *Sellers Market Report.* Monthly. Belmont, MA: Sellers Market Publishing.
Articles cover sales prospects and purchasing contacts in defense and high-tech industries.

Statistical Information

779. *Computer and Business Equipment Marketing and Forecast Data Book.* Hasbrouck Heights, NJ: Hayden Book Co., 1985. 156 p.
Prepared by the Computer and Business Equipment Manufacturers Assn., the data analyzes hardware and equipment manufacturing, employment, and other economic factors in the industry. Forecasts cover economic trends and domestic demand to 1990. The performance of the top 100 companies is also reviewed.

780. *Electronic Market Data Book.* Annual. Washington, DC: Electronic Industries Assn.
Detailed statistical information on production, sales, foreign trade, R&D, and U.S. government markets is based on information from several hundred companies, government, and private sources.

781. *Electronic News Financial Fact Book and Directory.* Annual. New York: Fairchild Books.
Business and financial information for various years covering 650 publicly owned electronic companies includes sales, stock information, individual firm organization, and financial data.

Associations

National Council of Technical Service Industries. 1850 K Street, N.W., Suite 1190, Washington, DC 20006.

Technical Marketing Society of America. 3711 Long Beach Blvd., Suite 609, Los Angeles, CA 90807.

Core Library Collection

ANNUALS

782. Sheth, Jagdish N., ed. *Research in Consumer Behavior.* Greenwich, CT: JAI Press, Inc.
Scholarly and state-of-the-art papers on consumer behavior are included in this series which is intended for monographic length papers that are too long for journal articles.

783. Sheth, Jagdish N., ed. *Research in Marketing: A Research Annual.* Greenwich, CT: JAI Press, Inc.
Original essays on new and significant research on various aspects of marketing are in each volume of this series.

784. Woodside, Arch G., ed. *Advances in Business Marketing: A Research Annual.* Annual. Greenwich, CT: JAI Press, Inc.
This annual illustrates the increasing attention business marketing is receiving as a theoretical and applied research topic. The lengthy empirical and theoretical, scholarly research papers and literature reviews cover a variety of issues in industrial and commercial marketing.

BIBLIOGRAPHIES

785. American Marketing Assn. *Bibliography Series.* Irregular. Chicago.
This is an important series for academic libraries. Recent publications in this series are listed by author in this bibliography.

786. *Annotated Bibliography of Secondary Sources for Bank Marketing Research.* Chicago: Information Center, Bank Marketing Assn., 1986. 28 p.
Data sources, fact books, directories, special issues of periodicals, and federal and local government information are included. Useful for locating statistical information, writing a marketing plan, and determining market share or competitive analysis.

787. Byerly, Greg, and Rubin, Richard E. *The Baby Boom: A Selective Annotated Bibliography.* Lexington, MA: Lexington Books, 1985. 238 p.
Books, dissertations, government publications, and journal articles cover demographics, economic, sociological, and psychological marketing perspectives concerning this demographic phenomenon.

788. Cooper, Philip D.; Jones, Karen M.; and Wong, John K. *An Annotated and Extended Bibliography of Health Care Marketing.* Chicago: American Marketing Assn., 1984. 186 p.

More than 600 articles, published from the late 1970s through 1984 are included in this bibliography. Double cross-references list an article by the marketing area such as market research or service development and also by the health care setting such as hospital or nursing home.

789. Dickson, John R. *The Bibliography of Marketing Research Methods.* 2d ed. Lexington, MA: Published for the Marketing Science Institute by Lexington Books, 1986. 788 p.

More than 9,000 entries for books, articles, handbooks, and conference proceedings are organized into three broad categories—marketing research function, data collection methods, and data analysis techniques. These are further subdivided by many headings and subheadings for specific subjects. An author and subject index are provided.

790. Fildes, Robert Dews, and David, Howell Syd. *A Bibliography of Business and Economic Forecasting.* New York: Facts on File, 1981. 424 p.

Journal articles from thirty journals and books published from 1971 to 1978, and a few important earlier references are included in this bibliography. The citations are indexed by some 500 topics for quick access to a specific subject. Some articles are labeled as basic or advanced to indicate the level of mathematical complexity. Material is useful for the manager, student, or academician.

791. Fisk, Raymond P., and Tansuhaj, Patriya S. *Services Marketing: An Annotated Bibliography.* Chicago: American Marketing Assn., 1985. 256 p.

More than twenty-one years of literature, from 1964 to 1983, are included in this bibliography which covers journal articles, conference proceedings, books, and dissertations. The 1,991 entries are arranged in two parts. Conceptual insights include areas such as marketing strategy for services, elements in the service mix, management issues. Part two is about ten service fields such as health care, financial, professional, travel and tourism, sports, education, and telecommunication services.

792. LaLonde, Bernard J. *Supplement to Bibliography on Logistics and Physical Distribution Management.* Annual. Oak Brook, IL: Council of Logistics Management.

This annual supplement updates the *Bibliography on Physical Distribution Management* originally published in 1967. References are to material published during the previous calendar year including books, journals, newsletters, and trade publications covering areas such as logistics concepts, legal sources, statistical techniques, cost analysis, regulatory reform, materials management, and logistics planning.

793. Robinson, Larry M., and Adler, Roy D. *Marketing Megawords: The Top 150 Books and Articles.* Westport, CT: Praeger, 1987. 211 p.

Summaries and evaluations of books that are judged to have the most impact on the the marketing discipline are included in this book. Forty-six selections are based on citation analysis, others are winning articles and articles frequently mentioned in anthologies or collections of classics. The summaries are alphabetically arranged by author, with separate indexes by author and title for books and articles, and by date of publication. The top twenty articles and books are ranked by citation frequency.

794. Ryans, Cynthia C. *Small Business; An Information Sourcebook.* Phoenix, AZ: Oryx Press, 1987. 286 p.

For the small business, this annotated bibliography covers all aspects of starting and operating a business, including chapters on advertising, public relations, franchising, marketing, sales, and strategic planning.

DICTIONARIES

795. Baker, Michael J., ed. *Macmillan Dictionary of Marketing and Advertising.* New York: Nichols Publishing Co., 1984. 217 p.
This is a general reference work and the more technical jargon associated with media and statistical marketing techniques is not included. The concise definitions, cross-references to related terms, and brief sketches of key concepts are intended for practitioners, managers in other fields, and students.

796. Bodian, Nat G. *Encyclopedia of Mailing List Terminology.* Winchester, MA: Bret Scot Press, 1986. 320 p.
Definitions of mailing list terms and phrases cover acquiring, renting, compiling, evaluating, testing, and updating mailing lists. Appendices cover rules, trade customs, software capabilities, database participation, and a mailing list chronology.

797. Cavinato, Joseph L. *Transportation-Logistics Dictionary.* Washington, DC: Traffic Service Corp., 1982. 323 p.
Definitions and explanations reflect the changes in transportation regulations, developments in the industry, cost impacts, and productivity concerns.

798. Dutka, Solomon, and Roshwalb, Irving. *A Dictionary for Marketing Research.* New York: Audits & Surveys, Inc., 1983. 73 p.
Selected technical words that make up the jargon of marketing research are included. Many of these terms are borrowed from other disciplines but have a different meaning when applied to marketing research. This is also true of the borrowed general usage words. Each page has two columns, one for the definition and the other for a citation to a publication that has a detailed discussion of the term.

799. Hart, Norman A., and Stapleton, John. *Glossary of Marketing Terms.* 2d ed. London: William Heineman, Ltd., 1981. 206 p.
Some of the more than 2,000 terms have descriptive explanations rather than definitive ones because many marketing terms have no accepted definition. Terms from other disciplines are included based on the frequency of use in marketing operations.

800. Imber, Jane, and Toffler, Betsy-Ann. *Dictionary of Advertising and Direct Mail Terms.* New York: Barron's Educational Series, 1987. 500 p.
Definitions of almost 3,000 terms used in television, radio, print, and direct mail advertising are included in this dictionary.

801. Ostrow, Rona, and Smith, Sweetman R. *The Dictionary of Retailing.* New York: Fairchild Publications, 1985. 256 p.
Terms and phrases for stores, shopping centers, merchandising, data processing, accounting, personnel management in retailing, direct marketing, mail order, and consumer behavior are defined in this nontechnical dictionary. Retail associations and capsule biographies of historical figures associated with retail marekting are also included.

802. Ott, J. Steven, and Shafritz, Jay M. *Facts on File Dictionary of Nonprofit Organization Management.* New York: Facts on File, 1986. 407 p.
Words, terms, phrases, processes, laws, and court cases as they apply to nonprofit organizations are included in this dictionary. Areas covered include accounting, business practices, labor relations, management theory, marketing, and public relations.

803. Shapiro, Irving J. *Dictionary of Marketing Terms.* 4th ed. Totowa, NJ: Littlefield, Adams & Co., 1981. 276 p.

The more than 5,000 entries in this edition include terms from the behavioral sciences and marketing research not included in previous editions. Numerous cross-references are provided.

804. Urdang, Laurence, ed. *Dictionary of Advertising.* Lincolnwood, IL: NTC Business Books, 1986. 209 p.

The more than 4,000 terms listed are special meaning words or the jargon in day-to-day use in advertising agencies and corporations. In addition, services, organizations, abbreviations, and acronyms are included.

DIRECTORIES

805. *Bradford's Directory of Marketing Research Agencies and Management Consultants in the United States and the World.* Annual. Fairfax, VA: Bradford's Directory of Marketing Research Agencies.

The more than 900 agencies and consultants included in this edition are arranged alphabetically by state or country. Indexes by type of marketing research, an alphabetical listing of agencies and key personnel, and a list of associations are provided.

806. *Broadcasting/Cablecasting Yearbook.* Annual. Washington, DC: Broadcasting Publications.

A directory of radio, TV stations, cable systems, satellites, programming, advertising, and marketing agencies handling major TV accounts. The "Television Marketplace" section defines each television marketplace in relation to the viewing audience in surrounding counties.

807. Darnay, Brigitte T., and Nimchuk, John. *Newsletters Directory.* 3d ed. Detroit, MI: Gale Research Co., 1987. 1,162 p.

The more than 8,000 newsletter entries are arranged in thirty-two subject chapters. Full bibliographical information also includes descriptive information and online availability. Four indexes provide title, publisher, subject, and format (hard copy, online, etc.) information.

808. *Direct Mail List Rates and Data.* Monthly. Wilmette, IL: Standard Rate & Data Service.

A directory of mailing list brokers, compilers, and managers; a classified listing of business direct mailing lists, co-op mailings, and package inserts; consumer and farm lists that are available for the direct mail industry.

809. *Directory of Online Databases.* Quarterly. New York: Quadra/Elsevier, 1987.

The quarterly issues of this directory supersede the previous issues to provide current information on more than 2,800 databases which are arranged alphabetically. Each entry includes basic information. Separation indexes are by subject, producer, online gateways/services, telecommunications, and a master index for all of these.

810. *Dun's Consultants Directory.* Annual. Parsippany, NJ: Dun's Marketing Service, 1986. 4,038 p.

More than 25,000 U.S. consulting firms in 200 specialties are listed alphabetically by company name. The usual directory information also includes annual sales, date company started, business description, other locations, and officers for each agency.

Indexes by geographic location for headquarters, branch offices, and business specialty are included.

811. *The Federal Data Base Finder.* 2d ed. Potomac, MD: Information USA, Inc., 1987. 368 p.
More than 4,000 free and fee-based databases are divided into three sections—those directly online through federal agencies, contractors, or centers; commercial databases containing government supplied data; and computer tapes sold by the federal government. Basic information about each includes the contact agency or producer.

812. Frankenstein, Diane Waxer, and Frankenstein, George. *Brandnames: Who Owns What.* New York: Facts on File, 1986. 457 p.
This guide names the company that ultimately owns a product or brand. For the more than 7,890 major U.S. consumer corporations, each entry includes a brief corporate history and a list of brand names. The largest foreign companies selling in the U.S. are also included. Product categories and a detailed index are provided.

813. *Gale Directory of Publications: An Annual Guide to Newspapers, Magazines, Journals and Other Periodicals.* Annual. Detroit, MI: Gale Research Co.
Formerly titled *Ayer Directory of Publications* and more recently *IMS Directory of Publications,* this directory includes expanded coverage of periodicals and newspapers published in the U.S. and Canada. The directory is geographically arranged by state and city and has alphabetical and classified indexes.

814. *Green Book: International Directory of Marketing Research Houses and Services.* Annual. New York: New York Chapter, American Marketing Assn.
The alphabetical arrangement of research organizations includes basic information and a description of the services offered. The five indexes provide access by company services, market/industry specialties, computer programs available, geographical arrangement of companies and names of principal personnel.

815. Gruber, Katherine. *Encyclopedia of Associations.* 21st ed. Detroit, MI: Gale Research Co., 1986. 4 vols.
Volume one, in two parts, is a comprehensive listing of national organizations classified by broad categories with seventeen points of information for each entry. Part three is the expanded *Name and Key Word Index* which also lists consultants, research, and information centers in other Gale reference publications. Volume two is a geographic and executive index. Volume three, *New Associations and Projects,* supplies information on new organizations. Volume four lists nonprofit organizations with international memberships.

816. *Handbook of Advertising and Marketing Services.* New York: Executive Communications.
A directory of services, consultants, and experts in all areas of marketing includes advertising, broadcasting, and communications. Each entry concisely summarizes the service experience, expertise, type of clients, performance records, and contact persons of the company. A listing by major and subcategories is provided.

817. Hoffman, Roger. *The Complete Software Marketplace 1984-85.* New York: Warner Books, 1984. 236 p.
Included in this directory are software buying companies, distributors, venture capital firms, lawyers with computer law experience, industry publications, consultants, market research organizations, and other individuals and groups who can assist the novice trying to market software.

818. Holtz, Herman. *Directory of Federal Purchasing Offices: Where, What, How to Sell to the U.S. Government.* New York: Wiley, 1981. 415 p.

Anyone interested in selling to the federal government will find this directory a source of information. In addition to agency addresses, an explanation of the procurement system and an indication of what is purchased by each procurement office is included. A glossary of terms and an index of products and services is also provided.

819. Hong, Alfred, ed. *MEI: Marketing Economics Key Plants: Guide to Industrial Purchasing Power.* New York: Marketing Economics Institute, 1984. 632 p.

A two-part directory that lists more than 40,000 plants with 100 or more employees by state, county, and by SIC number for each county. The second part lists companies by SIC numbers within each industry by state and county. Only the address, phone number, SIC number, and employment range is given. The plant listings make this a potentially useful marketing tool.

820. Huffman, Robert J., and Watkins, Mary Michele. *Research Services Directory.* 3d ed. Detroit, MI: Gale Research Co., 1987. 641 p.

More than 3,400 fee- or contract-based organizations that provide research services including data collection and design, forecasting, surveys, and statistical studies are arranged alphabetically. Geographic, personal name, and subject indexes are provided. Kept up to date by *Research Services Directory: Supplement* which lists newly formed research services.

821. *Irregular Serials & Annuals: An International Directory.* 12th ed. New York: Bowker, 1986. 1,899 p.

Worldwide in scope, more than 35,500 serials, annuals, continuations, conference proceedings, and other publications issued irregularly or less frequently than twice a year are alphabetically arranged by title, under 266 subject headings. A list of serials available online and a title index are provided.

822. Marlow, Cecilia Ann, and Thomas, Robert C., eds. *The Directory of Directories.* 4th ed. Detroit, MI: Gale Research Co., 1987. 2 vols. 1,727 p.

This new edition covers directories of all kinds including business and industrial directories, professional and scientific rosters, foreign directories, lists, and guides which are arranged in sixteen broad categories. The subject index contains more than 3,000 entries and numerous cross-references providing access to to specific subject information.

823. *The Medical and Healthcare Marketplace Guide: A Comprehensive Industrial Guide to the U.S. Medical and Health Care Marketplace.* Annual. Miami, FL: International Bio-Medical Information Service.

Detailed profiles of more than 4,400 public and private medical and health-related companies, including foreign-owned companies and subsidiaries, are listed. These cover manufacturers, dealers, distributors, importers, and exporters in 247 separate product/service classifications. Sales and market shares for the fifty product and service areas and rankings for the top 500 largest companies are included.

824. *Million Dollar Directory.* Annual. Parsippany, NJ: Dun's Marketing Services. 5 vols. 9,775 p.

Approximately 160,000 public and private U.S. businesses with an indicated net worth of over $500,000 are alphabetically arranged giving officers, lines of business, SIC numbers, approximate sales, and numbers of employees. Separate industry and geographic volumes are provided.

825. O'Brien, Jacqueline Wasserman, and Wasserman, Steven R., eds. *Statistics Sources*. 10th ed. Detroit MI: Gale Research Co., 1986. 2 vols. 2,014 p.
Arranged by more than 20,000 subjects, primary sources of national statistical data in American publications are listed. Principal statistical sources for each country in the world are also included.

826. *Progressive Grocers Marketing Guidebook: The Book of Supermarket Distributions*. Annual. New York: Progressive Grocer Publishing Co.
This directory divides retail and wholesale grocery companies into seven regions and includes statistics about the industry as a whole as well as regional data. Information about market areas in each state includes company buying data and personnel.

827. *Sheldon's Retail Directory of the United States and Canada and Phelon's Resident Buyers and Merchandise Brokers*. Annual. New York: Phelon, Sheldon & Marsar, Inc.
This directory lists department stores; chains and independent companies; women's, men's, and children's specialty stores; and variety and furniture stores. Entries are arranged geographically including the name and locations of stores, department buyers, merchandise and advertising managers, and purchasing agents. Another section lists resident buyers and merchandise brokers arranged alphabetically, including the lines of merchandise bought.

828. *Standard Directory of Advertisers*. Annual. Wilmette, IL: National Register Publishing Co.
A directory of more than 17,000 companies that advertise nationally are arranged by industry. Each entry includes officers, product names, advertising agency, media used, and the advertising budget for some of the companies. Trade name and alphabetical indexes are provided. The *Geographic Index* is a separate volume. *Ad-Change,* a biweekly publication, updates the basic volume, and the bimonthly *Supplement* cumulates this information in *Ad-Change.*

829. *Standard Directory of Advertising Agencies: The Advertising Red Book*. 3/yr. Wilmette, IL: National Register Publishing Co.
Approximately 4,800 advertising agencies are included in this directory. Each listing includes the usual directory information, lists association memberships, the area of specialization, and annual billings with breakdown by type of media and the accounts or companies serviced by the agency.

830. *Technology Transfer Directory: A Guide to Brokers, Seekers, Sellers, Facilitators, Databases, Directories, Organizations and Bibliographies in the Field of Technology Transfer*. Paoli, PA: GRQ, 1986. 330 p.
This directory provides information for anyone wanting to license, buy, market, or otherwise transfer technology between organizations. Sections on industries, universities, brokers, state and local development agencies, and research institutes provide additional information.

831. *Thomas Register of American Manufacturers and Thomas Register of Catalog Files*. New York: Thomas Publishing Co., 1986. 21 vols.
A detailed directory of products and services arranged by state, with separate volumes for an alphabetical listing of company profiles that give branch offices, asset ratings and company officials, two volumes of trademark and brand names, and an alphabetical listing of company catalogs.

832. Thomas, Robert C., ed. *Encyclopedia of Associations: Association Periodicals.* Annual. Detroit, MI: Gale Research Co. 3 vols.

More than 18,000 journals, magazines, bulletins, newsletters, directories, etc., which are published by trade associations, professional societies, and nonprofit organizations, are included in this directory. Arranged by broad subject categories, the descriptive entries include basic information. Subject, organization, name/acronym, publication, and title/keyword indexes are included. Volume one is *Business, Finance, Industry and Trade Publications.*

833. *Trademark Register of the United States.* Annual. Washington, DC: U.S. Patent Searching Service.

Currently in force and renewed trademarks registered in the U.S. Patent and Trademark Office are arranged by International Classification Schedule numbers for goods, products, and services. Expired registrations are not included.

834. *Ulrich's International Periodicals Directory: A Classified Guide to Current Periodicals, Foreign and Domestic.* 25th ed. New York: Bowker, 1986. 2 vols. 2,272 p.

A comprehensive list of periodicals, based on the Bowker International Serials Database, lists 68,000 periodicals in 534 subject areas, limited to periodicals issued more frequently than once a year and on a regular basis. Newspaper and government publications are omitted. Title and subject indexes are provided.

835. U.S. Small Business Administration. *U.S. Government Purchasing and Sales Directory: Guide for Selling and Buying in the Government Market.* Washington, DC: U.S. Government Printing Office, 1985. 191 p.

An alphabetical list of products and services purchased by civilian agencies and military department. Explanations of assistance in obtaining prime contracts and subcontracts and the market for research and development are included.

836. *Who Knows: A Guide to Washington Experts.* Washington, DC: Washington Researchers Publishing, 1986. 446 p.

This directory lists more than 10,000 specialists in Washington, DC who can help answer questions about industries, markets, products, or issues without charging a fee. Each is listed by name, title, address, and direct telephone number. A detailed index of 8,000 subject categories is provided.

837. Wood, Donna, ed. *Trade Names Dictionary.* 5th ed. Detroit MI: Gale Research Co., 1986. 2 vols. 1,818 p.

Trade, brand, product, designed, and coined names are alphabetically listed. Each entry gives the name, product description, company distributor's name, and a code to the source for this information. A supplement, *New Trade Names,* provides a list of new trade and company names.

838. Wood, Donna, ed. *Trade Names Dictionary: Company Index.* 5th ed. Detroit, MI: Gale Research Co., 1986. 2 vols. 1,838 p.

A companion to the *Trade Names Dictionary,* this is an alphabetical name and address list of the 41,000 companies in the basic volumes. For each company, the name of the product manufactured, marketed, or imported and a product description are given.

GUIDEBOOKS/HANDBOOKS

839. Allen, Randy L. *Bottom Line Issues in Retailing: The Touche Ross Guide to Retail Management.* Radnor, PA: Chilton Book Co., 1984. 294 p.
Some issues facing retailers are merchandise management, information processing, retail accounting, business planning, and store operations. The approach to these issues is quantitative. Identifying needed data, means of gathering data, and converting this information into action to increase productivity and profitability are some areas covered.

840. Beacham, Walton; Hise, Richard T.; and Tongren, Hale N. *Beacham's Marketing Reference.* Washington, DC: Research Publications, 1986. 2 vols. 1,045 p.
An alphabetical arrangement of 265 marketing concepts each of which is explained with examples that describe benefits, implementation, and evaluation of the importance of these terms to the success of the business. The explanations are written by marketing experts in jargon-free language.

841. Birnes, William, and Markman, Gary. *Selling at the Top: The 100 Best Companies to Sell for in America Today.* New York: Harper & Row, 1985. 338 p.
The five best companies in various areas of the service, consumer goods, and light and heavy industries are ranked by compensation, commission, support, and intangibles for salespeople.

842. Bly, Robert W. *Create the Perfect Sales Piece: How to Produce Brochures, Catalogs, Fliers and Pamphlets.* New York: Wiley, 1985. 242 p.
This do-it-yourself guide to producing promotional literature tells how to create printed material that fits a company's image and budget. Sample illustrations of various types of publications, visual aids, typefaces, art work, worksheets, and checklists are included.

843. Bobrow, Edwin E., and Bobrow, Mark David, eds. *Marketing Handbook.* Homewood, IL: Dow Jones-Irwin, 1985. 2 vols.
Volume one, *Marketing Practices,* is a state-of-the-art handbook in applied marketing covering areas such as consumer and industrial goods and services, international marketing, product life cycle, marketing research, and developing the marketing plan. How-to applications are included to help develop new approaches to marketing. Volume two, *Marketing Management,* has chapters on the role of the manager in planning, training, selection of distribution channels, organization of a department, measurement techniques, new product development, and the legal aspects of marketing. Each volume has its own subject and name index.

844. Bobrow, Edwin E., and Shafer, Dennis W. *Pioneering New Products: A Market Survival Guide.* Homewood, IL: Dow Jones-Irwin, 1987. 234 p.
This is a practical, goal-oriented guide for marketers, entrepreneurs, and "intrapreneurs" that covers a systematic approach to new product development and marketing.

845. Bobrow, Edwin E., and Wizenberg, Larry, eds. *Sales Manager's Handbook.* Homewood, IL: Dow Jones-Irwin, 1983. 522 p.
This state-of-the-art manual is a collection of articles written by authorities on topics that are relevant to the sales manager. These include an overview of sales management responsibilities, methods of selling goods, productivity, sales campaigns, training, development and compensation of sales-people, and the place of the sales force management in the company.

846. Bond, Robert E. *The Source Book of Franchise Opportunities.* Homewood, IL: Dow Jones-Irwin, 1985. 509 p.

The purpose of this book is to provide assistance in deciding which franchise meets an individual's needs, experience level, and financial position. The franchises are arranged in forty-four categories. Comparable information about the 1,400 listings includes financial data, services of the company, and a brief explanation of the organization. An index by category and an alphabetical listing are included.

847. Breen, George Edward, and Blankenship, Albert Breneman. *Do-It-Yourself Marketing Research.* 2d ed. New York: McGraw-Hill, 1982. 303 p.

A practical guide for the nonprofessional market researcher that explains how to conduct market studies necessary for making decisions in a small business, giving enough information so that the individual can decide when professional help is needed.

848. Britt, Steuart Henderson, and Guess, Norman F., eds. *Dartnell Marketing Manager's Handbook.* 2d ed. Chicago: Dartnell Corp., 1983. 1,293 p.

The most effective marketing principles are presented for developing a marketing plan that meets the competition, provides for long-range planning but is flexible enough for adjustment to constantly changing marketing conditions. Partial contents include organizing and staffing, establishing marketing objectives, and putting the marketing plan into action.

849. Buell, Victor P., ed. *Handbook of Modern Marketing.* 2d ed. New York: McGraw-Hill, 1986. 1,296 p.

Designed for marketing managers at all levels, each chapter is written by an expert in the field. A practical treatment of the major markets—consumer, industrial, service, and government—can be understood by the generalist. In addition to basic subjects, areas such as nonbusiness marketing, corporate identification, using marketing consultants, marketing control systems, and automatic retailing are included.

850. Cohen, William A. *How to Sell to the Government: A Step-by-Step Guide to Success.* New York: Wiley, 1981. 434 p.

Successful marketing to the federal government requires an understanding of the laws, regulations, rules, practices, procedures, or traditions that govern the purchasing process. This books covers a wide range of topics including the way the government does business, proposal writing, pricing, types of government contracts, and negotiations.

851. Daniells, Lorna M. *Business Information Sources.* rev. ed. Berkeley, CA: University of California Press, 1985. 673 p.

A comprehensive guide to sources for all types of business information that is needed by the business person, students, and librarians. Basic business sources, U.S. and foreign economic statistics and trends, industry statistics, sources for locating information on companies, organizations, and individuals are included. Each entry has a descriptive annotation. The detailed author, title, and subject index provides access to specific topics.

852. Davidow, William H. *Marketing High Technology: An Insiders View.* New York: Free Press, 1986. 194 p.

The differences of marketing high technology products as compared with consumer products is explained. The importance of marketing strategy, need for international markets, provision of services and pricing are some of the topics in this book.

853. Davidson, Jeffrey P. *Marketing to the Fortune 500 and Other Corporations.* Homewood, IL: Dow Jones-Irwin, 1986. 291 p.

Inside tips that will help a small business obtain contracts with large corporations for products and services includes a detailed plan for securing these contracts. Lists of purchasing offices, regional purchasing magazines, market research information sources, and state-sponsored support organizations are also included.

854. Dutka, Solomon; Frankel, Lester; and Roshwalb, Irving. *How to Conduct Surveys.* New York: Audits & Surveys, 1982. 197 p.

A step-by-step guide to planning and carrying out a survey project that covers many problems that arise in the collection, presentation, analysis, and interpretation of data. The establishment of survey objectives, sample selection, questionnaire design, interviewing techniques, analysis, and reporting the results are covered.

855. Fletcher, Alan D., and Bowers, Thomas A. *Fundamentals of Advertising Research.* 2d ed. Columbus, OH: Grid, 1983. 343 p.

A how-to book covering marketing research techniques, interpretations, and applications, including the methodology of advertising research, gathering data, selecting samples, conducting research, and writing the report.

856. Foote, Cameron S. *The Fourth Medium: How to Use Promotional Literature to Increase Sales and Profits.* Homewood, IL: Dow Jones-Irwin, 1986. 226 p.

Promotional literature can have an impact on marketing success, and this book covers every aspect of preparation and production from developing the concept to distribution.

857. *Franchise Opportunities Handbook.* Annual. Washington, DC: U.S. Department of Commerce, International Trade Administration and Minority Business Development Agency, U.S. Government Printing Office.

The introductory section contains general information on franchising, checklists, and other sources of information. The franchises are listed alphabetically including description, number in operation, equity needed, financial assistance available, training, and managerial assistance. A category index is provided.

858. Goldstucker, Jac L., ed. and Echemendia, Otto R., comp. and comps. *Marketing Information: A Professional Reference Guide.* 2d ed. Atlanta, GA: Business Publications Division, College of Business Administration, Georgia State University, 1987. 384 p.

The first part of this publication is an extensive directory of marketing associations, marketing research services, and consulting organizations, the largest advertising agencies, special libraries, and information centers, research centers, marketing education programs, and U.S. government agencies and organizations. The second part is an annotated bibliography of marketing books and periodicals that are arranged by marketing subjects and disciplines. Title, section, and publisher indexes are provided.

859. *A Guide to Marketing New Industrial and Consumer Products.* Englewood Cliffs, NJ: Prentice-Hall, 1985. 106 p.

Individuals involved with the introduction of new products will find this a flexible document, and usable as a checklist or timetable for the market plan. From the prototype testing through post evaluation, tasks are outlined, complete with guide pages, diagrams, graphs, and worksheets for each task section. A glossary of terms is also included.

860. Harper, Rose. *Mailing List Strategies: A Guide to Direct Mail Success.* New York: McGraw-Hill, 1986. 213 p.

The customer file is not only an important asset of direct mail marketing, but it is also a marketing decision support system. Because a constant development of new customers is necessary, this book covers information about list companies, renting lists, types of direct response lists, researching market potential, internal files, and list security.

861. Henry, Donald L. *The Profitable Professional Practice.* Englewood Cliffs, NJ: Prentice-Hall, 1985. 286 p.

Techniques for a more profitable professional practice for a number of professions are covered in this guide. Information provided will help reduce workload, and increase productivity as well as increase income. Some areas covered include office administration, site selection, expanding the practice, organizing a professional corporation, legal rights, and tax information. Forms, tables, and planning charts are provided.

862. Herpel, George L., and Slack, Steve. *Specialty Advertising: New Dimensions in Creative Marketing.* Irving, TX: Specialty Advertising Association, International, 1983. 188 p.

A scholarly and a practical approach provides a perspective on specialty advertising, explains what it is, and tells how and when to use it. Areas covered include the promotional mix, behavioral factors, promotion evaluation, developing image, motivating dealers, and building and maintaining market share.

863. Hodgson, Richard S. *The Dartnell Direct Mail and Mail Order Handbook.* 3d ed. Chicago: Dartnell Corp., 1980. 1,538 p.

A practical guide to developing a direct mail/mail order program that assists with planning and creating a producing campaign that is flexible and profitable. Checklists, reference data, successful ideas, testing for better results, sampling, couponing, and merging and purging mailing lists are a few of the areas covered.

864. Holtz, Herman. *Direct Marketer's Workbook.* New York; Wiley, 1986. 348 p.

A practical handbook that explains how to develop a successful sales campaign through the mails that includes worksheets and checklists to guide the marketer through product selection, concept development, market testing, production, order processing, and sales tracking.

865. Holtz, Herman, and Schmidt, Terry. *The Winning Proposal: How to Write It.* New York: McGraw-Hill, 1981. 381 p.

Proposal writing ability is essential for any company seriously pursuing governmental business. This book provides guidance in techniques and methods for writing winning proposals for federal, state, and local governments. Information covered includes types of contracts, statement of work, committee evaluations, common failures, proposal elements and formats, management plans, presentation strategies, and unsolicited proposals. A speciman proposal is included.

866. Johnson, Eugene M.; Scheuing, Eberhard E.; and Gaida, Kathleen A. *Profitable Service Marketing.* Homewood, IL: Dow Jones-Irwin, 1986. 303 p.

Intended for the service manager, this book analyzes the nature of service, the service environment, the management cycle, and the service marketing mix. Major issues and trends that confront the manager and the practical application of modern marketing concepts and practices are covered.

867. Kotler, Philip, and Andreasen, Alan R. *Strategic Market for Nonprofit Organizations.* 3d ed. Englewood Cliffs, NJ: Prentice-Hall, 1987. 560 p.
This book applies the conceptual system of marketing to the marketing problems of nonprofit organizations. In part one, the environment, the philosophy, and the basic concepts for targeting customer markets are discussed. Part two emphasizes strategic planning and organization. Part three covers conceptual tools for implementing detailed tactics and programs including the marketing mix.

868. Kotler, Philip, and Clarke, Roberta N. *Marketing for Health Care Organizations.* 2d ed. Englewood Cliffs, NJ: Prentice-Hall, 1987. 545 p.
The conceptual systems of marketing are applied to the marketing problems of health care and social service organizations. Organizing market research, analyzing market opportunities, planning the marketing mix, and supporting the marketing effort are covered.

869. Lee, Donald D. *Industrial Marketing Research: Techniques and Practices.* 2d ed. New York: Van Nostrand Reinhold, 1984. 208 p.
A practical guide for industrial marketing research that explains objectives, functions, processes, practices, and applications. Management needs for current and projected information on markets, customers, end users, competitors, new products, and business trends are covered. The organization, recruitment, and training of the market research staff are included.

870. Lemmon, Wayne A. *The Owner's and Manager's Market Analysis Workbook for Small to Moderate Retail and Service Establishments.* New York: AMACOM, 1980. 230 p.
Using the techniques outlined in this book, the small to moderate retail or service establishment owner can do basic market analysis to determine profitability of locating a business in a specific market location.

871. MacDonald, Charles R. *24 Ways to Greater Business Productivity: Master Checklist for Marketing, Advertising, Sales, Distribution, and Customer Service.* Englewood Cliffs, NJ: Institute for Business Planning, 1982. 446 p.
The detailed checklists and instructions are designed for ths marketing manager who wants to improve performance of marketing functions. Self-audits provide a means of rating each function, interpreting the rating, and knowing what to do next. Some areas covered include new product planning and development, market research, and analysis.

872. Makens, James C. *The Marketing Plan Workbook.* Englewood Cliffs, NJ: Prentice-Hall, 1985. 204 p.
A practical planning book that has ready-to-use forms, tables, and worksheets that assist in organizing everything involved in market planning. Practical guidance is supplied for handling each step of the plan and suggestions for avoiding potential problem areas are included.

873. McMahon, Robert J. *Bank Marketing Handbook: How to Compete in the Financial Services Industry.* Boston: Bank Publishing Co., 1986. 339 p.
A guide to productive methods and techniques for marketing products and services of commercial banks. Includes charts, worksheets, and checklists, most of which are easily programmed for personal computers or mainframes.

874. Miller, Robert B., and Heiman, Stephen. *Strategic Selling: The Unique Sales System Proven Successful by America's Best Companies.* New York: William Morrow, 1985. 319 p.
This book covers the "Win-Win" approach to selling which is concerned with the customer's needs. The basic elements of strategic selling are covered along with the

multiaccount strategies of managing your time, focusing on the customer, and developing an action plan.

875. Pope, Jeffery L. *Practical Marketing Research.* New York: AMACOM, 1981. 269 p.
Focus is on the application of marketing research techniques to problems, real-world issues, or how to get things done by providing information for those responsible for the research function. Some areas covered include packaging, advertising, sales testing, and product concept.

876. Riso, Ovid. *Sales Promotion Handbook.* 7th ed. Chicago: Dartnell Corp., 1979. 1,206 p.
A practical compilation that explains ideas, methods, and techniques for developing and evaluating the success of a sales promotion plan. Coverage includes organization, budgeting, sales leads, customer service, trade shows, motivating salespeople, and public relations. Examples, illustrations, and charts are supplied. Lists of business directories and publications are a part of this desk reference handbook.

877. Robeson, James F., and House, Robert G. *The Distribution Handbook.* New York; Free Press, 1985. 970 p.
Those interested in distribution will find this reference book has practical, how-to information on a wide variety of topics. The material applies to all levels of distribution—products, wholesaler, and retailer—with emphasis on the total-channel or producer's perspective.

878. Rogers, Robert S., and Chamberlain, V. B. *National Account Marketing Handbook.* New York: AMACOM, 1981. 292 p.
All aspects of national account marketing are covered from definitions and identification of the characteristics of the national account to the legal and international aspects of selling to the federal government.

879. Seltz, David D. *Handbook of Innovative Marketing Techniques.* Reading MA: Addison-Wesley, 1981. 329 p.
The practical and economical marketing and sales techniques included in this book cover sales promotion, new sales, advertising concepts, image building, administration, finance, and examples of sales and collection letters.

880. Simon, Julian L. *How to Start and Operate a Mail-Order Business.* 4th ed. New York: McGraw-Hill, 1987. 547 p.
A step-by-step approach to starting a mail order business that teaches the business as well as outlining the decisions that must be made. Facts and data about the business, poducts that sell, strategies, testing, advertising costs, and use of the computer are some of the areas covered.

881. Stansfield, Richard H. *The Dartnell Advertising Manager's Handbook.* 3d ed. Chicago: Dartnell Corp., 1982. 1,088 p.
The practical information in this publication covers 2,600 separate subjects and contains over 500 illustrations, case histories of ad campaigns, creative copy, tips on choosing the right media, planning a budget, and more.

882. Stone, Bob. *Successful Direct Marketing Methods.* 3d ed. Chicago: Crain Books, 1984. 496 p.
A practical book that has a sound conceptual base and covers areas such as direct marketing research, use of direct marketing in the marketing mix and strategic business planning. Basics such as start-up procedures, selection of merchandise, choosing the media, and producing direct mail packages that work are thoroughly explained.

883. Taylor, James W. *Competitive Marketing Strategies.* Radnor, PA: Chilton Book Co., 1986. 184 p.

A step-by-step plan to develop and execute profitable market strategy that covers areas such as product life cycles; measuring and analyzing market share and competitive advantage, cost, and prices; refining marketing strategies; and measuring progress.

884. U.S. Patent and Trademark Office. *Patent and Trademark Forms Booklet.* Washington, DC: U.S. Government Printing Office, 1979. ca. 350 leaves.

These full-size, reproducible forms of frequently used patent and trademark applications are those used in filing patent and trademark cases. The law does not require the use of these or any other particular forms as long as the individual complies with the requirements set forth in the laws. The forms can be modified to fit a particular situation. Translations of twenty-three foreign languages for some of the oath and declaration forms needed in other countries are also included.

885. Vichas, Robert P. *Complete Handbook of Profitable Marketing Research Techniques.* Englewood Cliffs, NJ: Prentice-Hall, 1982. 432 p.

Forty basic marketing research techniques that are practical, productive, and economical for even the smallest companies include applications, forms, checklists, and questionnaires.

886. Weilbacher, William M. *Choosing an Advertising Agency.* Chicago: Crain Books, 1983. 170 p.

Whether changing agencies or hiring one for the first time, this guide explains how to establish a search group, write an account profile, determine selection criteria, develop a fact sheet, and evaluate agency presentations.

887. Wizenberg, Larry, ed. *The New Products Handbook.* Homewood, IL: Dow Jones-Irwin, 1986. 337 p.

From planning through development, research, and evaluation, the techniques and strategies suggested provide for a successful introduction of a new product. Marketing and new product managers, entrepreneurs and managers of small businesses can benefit from this information.

888. Woy, James, ed. *Encyclopedia of Business Information Sources: A Bibliographic Guide to Approximately 22,000 Citations Covering More Than 1,100 Primary Subjects of Interest to Business Personnel.* 6th ed. Detroit, MI: Gale Research Co., 1986. 878 p.

The subjects are arranged alphabetically, and each has a list of general works, abstracts, indexes, bibliographies, directories, encyclopedias, financial ratios, handbooks, databases, periodicals, and associations. Citations to the correct or related topics are included. *Encyclopedia of Business Information Sources: Supplement* updates this publication and provides new sources of business information.

INDEXES

889. *American Statistics Index: A Comprehensive Guide and Index to Statistical Publications of the U.S. Government.* Monthly with annual cumulations. Bethesda, MD: Congressional Information Service, Inc.

This is the best source for most of the statistical publications of government agencies, congressional committees, and statistics-producing programs. A detailed subject index, category, geographic area, title of report, and report indexes are provided. The numbers in the indexes refer to the abstract number which has a complete description of the publication and details about the statistical data. The

Superintendant of Documents number is also given. Microfiche copy of many of the items is a part of the service.

890. *Business Periodicals Index.* 11/yr. with annual cumulations. New York: H.W. Wilson Co.
This is the basic business index found in most college, university, and public libraries that provides a detailed subject index to approximately 300 selected business periodicals. An author listing of book reviews appearing in the indexed periodicals is at the end of each issue.

891. *Predicasts F&S Index: United States.* Weekly with quarterly and annual cumulations. Cleveland, OH: Predicasts, Inc.
Over 1,000 sources, including magazines, newspapers, government reports, and other relevant business publications, are indexed in two volumes. One volume is indexed by the modified SIC number listed in the front of the volume by product/service name. The other volume is alphabetical by company name.

892. *Statistical Reference Index: A Selective Guide to American Statistical Publications from Private Organizations and State Government Sources.* Monthly with annual culumations. Washington, DC: Congressional Information Service.
Publications of associations, business and independent research organizations, state governments, and universities are indexed by subjects, names, categories, issuing sources, and titles. The index section provides the item number for location of the abstract of the information. Microfiche copy of many of the items is a part of this publication. A good source for marketing information.

893. *Wall Street Journal Index; Barron's Index.* Monthly with annual cumulations. New York: Dow Jones.
The *Wall Street Journal* volume of the index has separate listings for corporate and general news. The *Barron's* volume combines corporate, general news, and authors in one listing. Brief summaries in chronological order accompany the citations in both volumes.

PERIODICALS

894. *Advertising Age.* Semiweekly. Chicago: Crain Communications, Inc.
The basic trade journal for the advertising and marketing industry covers topics such as advertising expenditures, finances of advertising agencies, and consumer recall of advertising. Data are from company reports, trade associations, and private research firms. Annual tables and market shares for some products such as coffee, cold cereal, liquor, and wine are also included.

895. *American Demographics.* 10/yr. Ithaca, NY: American Demographics, Inc.
Articles on all aspects of demography include developments, analyses, population shifts, trends, and data sources.

896. *American Journal of Small Business.* Quarterly. Baltimore, MD: University of Baltimore.
Articles of a theoretical or practical nature are intended for academicians, consultants, government officials, and others who support the small business community.

897. *The American Salesman: The National Magazine for Sales Professionals.* Monthly. Burlington, IA: National Research Bureau, Inc.
The articles cover a range of topics and give practical advice for the salesperson whether a beginner or an experienced individual. Many are motivational in nature.

898. *Bank Marketing: Publication of the Bank Marketing Assn.* Monthly. Chicago: The Association.

Articles on marketing techniques that are useful to the banking industry cover a wide variety of topics. Examples of advertising campaigns are included. The July issue contains a "Directory of Bank Marketing Services" categorized for locating supplies in each service area.

899. *Business Marketing.* Monthly. Chicago: Crain Communications, Inc.

This business-to-business marketing magazine includes news and articles on strategy and tactics and has an annual listing of business/industrial advertising agencies. A monthly column, "Marketing Information," lists new marketing studies and directories.

900. *Chilton's Distribution for Traffic and Transportation Decision Makers.* Monthly. Radnor, PA: Chilton Co.

A trade journal for the manager in charge of physical distribution covering current developments in distribution and management for all types of freight and traffic. The *Intermodal Guide* in the July issue is a directory of trucking lines, ports, ocean carriers, transportaion and distribution equipment, and public warehouses.

901. *Commerce Business Daily.* Daily. Washington, DC: U.S. Department of Commerce.

A Monday through Friday publication that lists U.S. government procurement invitations for services and supplies, contract awards, subcontracting leads, surplus property sales, and foreign business opportunities. Detailed descriptions of each item include the contact person.

902. *Computer & Electronics Marketing.* Monthly. New York: A/S/M Communications.

Interpretive news reports, case histories, and analysis of trends and marketing strategy are included in this tabloid format.

903. *Direct Marketing Magazine.* Monthly. Garden City, NY: Hoke Communications.

Included in this publication is information about the use of mailing lists; direct response advertising used by various businesses such as manufacturers, retailers, wholesalers, banks, and insurance companies; and reports on the use of new technology with its impact on direct marketing.

904. *Franchising World.* Quarterly. Washington, DC: International Franchise Assn.

Current information on franchising covers trends, developments, operations, management, public relations, and interviews with franchisors.

905. *Health Marketing Quarterly.* Quarterly. New York: Haworth Press, Inc.

Each issue is devoted to a different health, human service, or delivery system. The articles, from educators and practitioners, provide administrators of health care with a framework for assisting them in marketing their services.

906. *Journal of Advertising.* Quarterly. Laramie, WY: College of Commerce and Industry, University of Wyoming.

This scholarly journal of the American Academy of Advertising focuses on theoretical developments in the psychological and philosophical aspects of communication and the relationship of these to advertising.

907. *Journal of Advertising Research.* Bimonthly. New York: Advertising Research Foundation.

Intended for users and practitioners of advertising research, this publication focuses on advertising research and methodology. Reports of findings rather than theoretical discussions and studies that are not based on student samples are included.

908. *The Journal of Business & Industrial Marketing.* Quarterly. Santa Barbara, CA: Grayson Associates.

A publication for professional marketers and academicians that includes articles on research, cases, concepts, industry reviews, and practices that can be utilized in business situations.

909. *Journal of Business Logistics.* Semiannual. Oak Brook, IL: National Council of Physical Distribution Management.

A blend of theoretical and practical material covering new information on logistics operations and management, emerging theory and tehcniques, and researched thought and practice in related areas of logistics management.

910. *Journal of Consumer Marketing.* Quarterly. Santa Barbara, CA: Grayson Associates.

Articles aimed at the marketing practitioner are concerned wtih new ideas applicable to marketing situations. The basis may be research or case studies of buyer behavior, marketing research, management, and marketing theory.

911. *Journal of Consumer Research: An Interdisciplinary Quarterly.* Quarterly. Los Angeles: Journal of Consumer Research, Inc.

Nearly a dozen scholarly associations sponsor this journal. The articles are interdisciplinary, empirical research on consumer behavior and processes that lead to the purchase of goods or services, including advertising.

912. *Journal of Data Collection: A Publication of Applied Marketing Research.* Semiannual. Chicago: Marketing Research Assn.

An important source for applied marketing research information that includes articles and interviews focusing on the latest technology and information.

913. *Journal of Forecasting.* Quarterly. New York: Wiley.

A scholarly journal covering all areas of forecasting including new products, technology, production, and finances. The articles may be methodology evaluation or practical applications to business or government.

914. *Journal of Health Care Marketing.* Quarterly. Chicago: American Marketing Assn.

For the practitioner and the academic, this journal is a bridge between the developing of marketing theories and the practical application of these theories to the various areas of health care marketing. Abstracts of pertinent articles on health care marketing are also included.

915. *Journal of Marketing.* Quarterly. Chicago: American Marketing Assn.

Serving as a bridge between the scholarly and practical approach, articles cover topics such as consumer behavior, business marketing, marketing theory, and strategic market planning. Interest is in new ideas or suggestions of new concepts instead of information on the present state of the art. "Marketing Literature Review" is a briefly annotated list of journal articles from the ABI/Inform database.

916. *Journal of Product Innovation Management.* Quarterly. New York: North-Holland.

Articles on theoretical structures and practical techniques are intended for the product manager involved with innovation and also for the student. The articles are based on empirical research, management observations and experience, and state-of-the-art reviews of issues.

917. *Journal of Retailing.* Quarterly. New York: Institute of Retail Management, New York University.

Some areas covered in this scholarly journal include buyer behavior, organization behavioral theory, and computers. The "Executive Summary" section provides the retailer with a practical, concise report of the theoretical articles that interest academicians.

918. *Journal of Small Business Management.* Quarterly. Morgantown, WV: Bureau of Business Research, West Virginia University.

All aspects of small business are covered with each issue devoted to a specific topic.

919. *Journal of the Academy of Marketing Science.* Quarterly. Coral Gables, FL: Academy of Marketing Science, School of Business Administration, University of Miami.

A scholarly journal that includes research articles on areas such as buyer behavior, retailing, wholesaling, marketing, management, research and forecasting, channels of distribution, pricing, sales management, and industrial marketing.

920. *Marketing & Media Decisions.* Monthly. New York: Decisions Publications, Inc.

A practically oriented magazine that has feature articles covering print and electronic media, special reports on marketing a variety of products, advertising expenditures by products, and media cost forecasts. A special issue is devoted to the top market success of the year.

921. *Marketing Communications.* Monthly. New York: Media Horizons, Inc.

Feature articles cover market planning and strategy, advertising, media, retailing, telemarketing, and direct marketing. Surveys such as *Product Profile Fact Book, Advertising and Promotional Expenditures,* and *Marketing Services Yearbook* are included in special issues.

922. *Marketing News.* Biweekly. Chicago: American Marketing Assn.

This newspaper covers what's new in marketing with articles written by staff and marketing professionals, both educators and business people. Several special issues each year cover topics such as marketing research, technology for marketing, and marketing education.

923. *Marketing Science.* Quarterly. Providence, RI: Institute of Management Science and Operations Society of America.

A scholarly journal that publishes quantitatively oriented marketing papers on theory development, marketing models, measurement, and applications. Also included are reviews of the latest trends in disciplines of interest to marketing—behavioral choice models, economic choice models, decision analysis. State-of-the-art academic papers on key issues of current interest in marketing are also published.

924. *Packaging.* Monthly. Boston: Cahners Publishing Co.

Developments, trends, and forecasts in the industry cover manufacturing, marketing, and R&D. Special issues are the *Annual Buyer's Guide* and the *Packaging Encyclopedia & Yearbook* which can be purchased separately.

925. *Potentials in Marketing.* 9/yr. Minneapolis, MN: Lakewood Publications, Inc.

Trends in marketing, sales ideas and promotions, advertising, and management techniques are covered. Conference reports, information on training programs, and incentive plans are also included.

926. *Sales & Marketing Management.* Monthly. New York: Bill Communications, Inc.

This is the most important magazine for all areas of sales and marketing that covers ideas, techniques, trends, and predictions for areas such as sales promotion, test marketing, managing costs, telemarketing, sales training and recruiting, motivation, and compensation. Four special issues are *Survey of Selling Costs* (February issue); *Survey of Industrial & Commercial Buying Power* (April issue); and the two-part series of *Survey of Buying Power* (July and October issues) which covers consumer and retail statistical data.

927. *Stores: The Magazine for the Retail Executive.* Monthly. New York: National Retail Merchants Assn.

A trade journal covering information on a variety of retail stores and products. Special features are listings of the 100 top specialty chains, top retail ads, top radio and TV ads, and the best store displays.

928. *Zip Target Marketing: The Magazine of Communications, Lists, Mailing Fulfillment.* Monthly. Philadelphia, PA: North American Publishing Co.

Intended for the direct mail executive, the focus is on articles discussing the use of direct mail and telemarketing techniques.

PROCEEDINGS

929. American Marketing Assn. *Educator's Proceedings.* Annual. Chicago: American Marketing Assn.

These are not a part of a numbered series, but they are essential for large academic libraries.

930. American Marketing Assn. *Proceedings.* Irregular. Chicago: American Marketing Assn.

This series is essential for academic libraries. Each is cataloged separately and is listed by author in this bibliography.

931. *Developments in Marketing Science.* Annual. Coral Gables, FL: Academy of Marketing Science, School of Business Administration, University of Miami.

This publication is a collection of papers presented at the annual conference of the Academy of Marketing Science. Contemporary marketing topics such as consumer behavior, business marketing, marketing management, marketing of services, and research methods are some areas covered.

STATISTICAL INFORMATION

932. *Ad$ Summary.* Quarterly with annual cumulations. New York: Leading National Advertisers.

The top 1,000 companies are ranked by total dollars spent on seven media, and by dollars spent on the separate media, which include magazines, newspaper supplements, network television, spot television, network radio, outdoor advertising, and cable TV networks. Also has alphabetical lists by brand names, with parent company name and the dollars spent by that brand for advertising.

933. *County Business Patterns.* Annual. Washington, DC: U.S. Bureau of the Census, U.S. Government Printing Office.

Separate issues for each state and a U.S. summary list for each four-digit SIC number, county totals of number of employees, taxable payrolls, and number of establishments by employment size. Useful for analyzing market potential, but the figures are not up to date.

934. Editor & Publisher Co. *Market Guide.* Annual. New York.

Demographic and business data for more than 1,600 U.S. and Canadian daily newspaper cities are arranged alphabetically by city within the state or province. Metropolitan Statistical Area rankings are included.

935. *Electronic Market Data Book.* Annual. Washington, DC: Electronic Industries Assn.

Detailed statistical information on production, sales, foreign trade, R&D, and U.S. government markets is based on information from several hundred companies, government, and private sources.

936. *Predicasts Basebook.* Annual. Cleveland, OH: Predicasts, Inc.

Coverage includes about fourteen years with approximately 28,000 series arranged by modified SIC number covering production, consumption, sales, wholesale price, plant, and equipment. The average yearly growth rate is also given.

937. *Predicasts Forecasts.* Quarterly cumulations. Cleveland, OH: Predicasts, Inc.

Short- and long-range forecasts that cover economic indicators, industries, products, and services are from a wide variety of printed sources. These are arranged by modified SIC numbers with the source of the forecast included.

938. *Rand McNally Commercial Atlas and Marketing Guide.* Annual. Chicago: Rand McNally & Co.

This atlas has economic and geographical information that includes statistical data and interpretations for business usage. ZIP code marketing data tables, maps of trading areas, of retail sales, of manufacturing, and MSA areas with accompanying statistical tables are included. Data tables for every county in the U.S. cover population, household and retail sales, and wholesale trade statistics. Useful for regional market studies.

939. *Sourcebook of Demographics and Buying Power for Every Zip Code in the USA.* Annual. Arlington, VA: CACI.

Data for this publication are based on CACI's geodemographic database which is updated annually to include proprietary current year estimates and five-year projections. The residential section, divided by state, includes demographic and socioeconomic profiles for each ZIP code in numerical order. The business section lists ZIP codes in numerical sequence, including information on the number of firms, estimated employment, and ranking by top five SIC numbers.

940. *Standard & Poor's Industry Surveys.* Quarterly. New York: Standard & Poor's Corp.

General information on various industries with composite industry data and statistics, market activity, company analyses and specific product segmentation. The *Trends and Projections* section analyzes the U.S. economy and includes forecasts for various economic indicators.

941. *The Survey of Buying Power Data Service.* Annual. New York: Sales & Marketing Management, Bill Publications.

Included in this loose-leaf compilation of demographic, economic, and sales data are detailed population characteristics, household income, buying income, retail sales by twelve store groups, ten merchandise lines, market data, and metropolitan/county market projections for population, income, and retail sales. The information is organized by geographic region, state, metropolitan area, county, and TV market area, with summary and ranking tables.

942. *Survey of Current Business.* Monthly. Washington, DC: Bureau of Economic Analysis, U.S. Government Printing Office.

An important source for business statistics. The monthly covers general business indicators and statistics on various products. A biennial supplement *Business Statistics* is a historical record of statistics in the monthly issues.

943. *Survey of Selling Costs.* Annual. New York: Bill Publications, Inc.

This compilation of selling facts and figures includes the "Selling Cost Index" and "Cost Per Sales Call" estimates for leading metro markets. The markets with the highest and lowest sales costs are noted. The information helps in determining and controlling selling expenses such as sales training, meetings, travel and entertainment, and other sales-support activities.

944. U.S. Bureau of Domestic Commerce. *Franchising in the Economy.* Annual. Washington, DC: U.S. Government Printing Office.

The first section is an explanation of the survey results covering trends, outlook, company characteristics, minority franchisees, and dominant types of franchises. The tables and charts, which are more than half of the publication, have data on sales, number of establishments, rankings by type of franchise, and information on specific franchises.

945. U.S. Department of Commerce. *Statistical Abstract of the United States.* Annual. Washington, DC: U.S. Government Printing Office.

A handy compilation of statistics covering most areas of the U.S. economy, including demographics, labor, business enterprises, transportation, manufacturing, and communications. Sources for the tables are given which is useful for locating additional information. Some tables have historical series.

946. *U.S. Industrial Outlook.* Annual. Washington, DC: Bureau of Industrial Economics, Department of Commerce, U.S. Government Printing Office.

This publication provides information on recent trends and the outlook for five years in advance for several hundred manufacturing and service industries. Statistical information covers the current situation, price, markets, and long-term prospects. No specific company information is included.

Author Index

Title Index

Subject Index

accounting services marketing, 750, 754, 759–60
advertisers directory, 302, 828
advertising account profile, 316, 886
advertising agency directory, 66, 301, 303, 829, 858
advertising agency evaluation, 316, 886
advertising budget, 314, 881
advertising costs, 683
advertising expenditures, 99, 303, 317, 331, 338–39, 342, 894, 920–21, 932
advertising psychological response, 337
advertising research, 308, 329, 855, 907
advertising services, 299–300, 816
advertising techniques, 187, 190, 314, 683, 881
advertising theory, 324, 328, 906
aging, 398, 400
apparel by mail, 460
apparel stores, 599, 601, 629
architectural services marketing, 752
Area of Dominant Influence (ADI), 341
association publications, 91, 118, 815
attitude research, 233, 257

baby boom, 395
bank advertising, 711
bank deposit services pricing, 715
bank marketing research, 709, 716, 718, 786
bank marketing techniques, 719–21
banking products, 713, 717, 873
beverage marketing statistics, 627
Black media, 294
Black-owned business, 54, 62
body language, 549
brand advertising, 113
brand differentiation, 506

brand management, 285, 488
brand marketing, 504, 687
brand names, 61, 132, 496, 498, 500–01, 506, 812, 831, 837
broadcasting industry directory, 295, 806
business analysis, 65, 67
business direct marketing, 427, 451, 467, 476
business forecasting, 120, 122, 172–73, 790, 913
business marketing communications, 363, 375
business organizations directories, 45, 117–19, 315, 421
business rankings, 52–53
business software directory, 126–30
business-to-business advertising, 349, 363, 453, 903
business-to-business catalogs, 366, 432
buyers' guides, 92

cable advertising, 310
chain stores, 596, 601, 612
channels of distribution, 72, 98, 108, 114, 346, 571, 590, 659, 843, 919
charities marketing, 751
citation analysis, 10
closing sales, 556
commercial bank marketing, 712, 718
commercial traffic executives, 573
communication process, 284
community health services, 728
company addresses, 29, 51, 54–56, 59, 61, 301–02, 824, 831
company branch locations, 214
company plant locations, 348, 819
competitive bidding, 141
competitive selling, 364
competitor intelligence, 234, 245, 359